OVERCOMING
TEMPTATION

OVERCOMING
TEMPTATION

By Larry Arrowood

Woodsong Publishing
Seymour, Indiana

Overcoming Temptation

By Larry Arrowood

2013

This is a revision, originally printed in 1986 by Word Aflame Press, Hazelwood, MO.

Reprinted by permission

All Scripture quotations are from the King James Version of the Bible unless otherwise identified.

Woodsong Publishing
7100 Persimmon Lake Drive
Seymour, IN 47274

www.woodsongpublishing.com

Cover design by Move My Church Media www.movemychurch.com
Printed in the United States of America.

ISBN 978-0-9892291-5-9

Table of Contents

CHAPTER 1

The Lion's Roar

I'm glad you've selected this book. Regretfully the subject matter is not one of those inspiring, mountain peak, and revelatory Christian topics like "Tapping Into God's Abundant Riches Now." In contrast, the title sounds a bit forlorn and could well be a turnoff, causing delay in diving into the subject matter. Whether the text is relevant at the moment is inconsequential, for your situation can change without notice. Like as with Job of old, the gales of adversity appear abruptly, and nothing you do can prevent them. My hope, even if you're sensing no immediate inclination for the subject, is that you read on anyway. Whether for yourself or for someone with whom you associate, you will find the topic of this book meaningful sooner than not. In the chapters ahead we'll survey mankind's age-old constant companion. Ironically, this companion is not a colleague of choice. Conversely, this companion is an intruder of ultimate magnitude, a prowler of devastating potential. It is one of the adversary's most effective tools: temptation. Like a bloodthirsty tick, this culprit will eventually find and attach itself to you. It's my desire to help equip you for that frightening moment. There are a dozen ways to deal with ticks, right and wrong. The same is true for dealing with temptation.

When we think of temptation we tend to stereotype both the predator and the prey. The former is generally associated with sensual lusts: pornography, wealth, or a flirtatious secretary. We overlook and downplay what we assume to be minor temptations: to cheat on our taxes, to conveniently share half-truths, to harbor bitterness. The prey is often considered one who is vulnerable due to inherent weaknesses or is lax in spiritual progress. So the new Christian is a target of Satan while the battle-scarred spiritual warrior is exempted. Our assumptions regarding the predator and prey are incomplete. Satan's tactics with temptation aren't relegated to any age group, don't exempt any social background, and have overwhelmed many at every level of spiritual development. No one, at any place or time, receives immunity. Noah, the preacher of righteousness, saved the world by obeying God, but he succumbed to the temptation of wine. Young David slew a giant with a slingshot and single stone, but as king he adhered to Satan's deception and numbered Israel. Solomon, the wisest of them all, capitulated to the pleas of his heathen wives (who were probably illiterate) and allowed idolatry into Israel. Young Demas forsook his missionary endeavor to follow the lure of the world.

Temptation is a devastating foe which often attacks when one is least expecting and in some cases flees before it can be properly identified. Temptation leaves the sincere, the novice, and the naïve with an utter sense of failure: humiliated, shuttering with horrible condemnation, and sometimes convinced that sin has been committed. The tempter amplifies condemnation, and guilt from just being tempted wields crushing blows, which often render the tempted so overwhelmed they yield to sin out of a sense of failure and hopelessness.

Overcoming Temptation is designed to help you in four areas. First, you need to recognize your temptation is not sin; in contrast, temptation is the unprovoked assault of the adversary. If you failed to lock the door to your home and during the night an intruder enters through the unlocked door and robs the house, are you guilty of a crime? Even though you left the door unlocked, you are not to blame for the actions of the intruder. You may somewhat second-guess the consequences of your absentmindedness, but you are not to blame for the actions of the thief. The theft was not of your doing.

Second, once you are tempted, you are able to defeat the tempter. In comparing temptation and sin, you cannot stop birds from flying overhead, but you can certainly keep those same birds from building a nest in your hair. Once tempted you must make proper efforts to combat the temptation. Further, we'll explore directives to put in place as preemptive strategies against inevitable attacks of the adversary.

Thirdly, you need to identify weaknesses of the flesh that make you vulnerable to the adversary. There's often a backstory to vulnerability: mental abuse, molestation, poor mentoring, instilled fears, learned helplessness, no prayer and Bible reading disciplines. It's sad, but statistics reveal a lot of repetitive behavioral failures. It's important to identify these weak areas and shore up the faulty foundation.

Finally, the Bible offers instruction regarding disciplines essential to battle against personal weaknesses and against direct satanic attacks of the soul.

A few years ago I became extremely perplexed by the spiritual defeat of some very sincere Christian friends. Because of their sincerity, I deduced that either the Scripture is weak in the area of directives regarding temptation or else these Christians lacked in basic understanding of what the Scripture says about overcoming temptation or else failed to apply these directives to their lives. It doesn't take much study of Scripture to eliminate the former as the reason for failures. From the study of Scripture we know God is concerned about the welfare of His creation. God's infallible Word covers the area of spiritual warfare. The problem involves the believer's concepts and actions regarding temptation: knowledge regarding temptation is limited, preemptive strategies are nonexistent, and the practice of spiritual disciplines is lacking or at best sporadic.

Sincerity is certainly a Christian trait, but it is not listed as an effective spiritual weapon or armor necessary to offset the barbed arrows of temptation. Satan scoffs at the cardboard shield of sincerity. He laughs at the flimsy sword of sincerity. The shock of seeing sincere Christians' lives shattered by yielding to the tempter made me evaluate some assumptions and search the Scriptures for a tangible answer. My conclusion? There is no way to cage the lion-like tenaciousness of temptation. Instead, we must train ourselves through study of Scripture and the practice of spiritual disciplines to be lion tamers. The Scripture describes the tempter as a roaring lion and admonishes the believer on how to respond: "Be sober, be vigilant; because your adversary the devil, as a roaring lion, walketh about, seeking whom he may devour: Whom resist stedfast in the faith…" (I Peter 5:8-9). Eugene Peterson shares an insightful paraphrase: "Keep a cool head. Stay alert. The Devil is poised to pounce, and would like nothing better than to catch you napping. Keep your guard up."[1] I like the African proverb, which well describes the law of survival. "Every day in Africa a gazelle wakes up. It knows it must run faster than the fastest lion or it will be killed. Every morning a lion wakes up. It knows that it must outrun the slowest gazelle or it will starve to death. It doesn't matter whether you are a lion or a gazelle. When the sun comes up, you better be running."[2]

The lion roars, but you do not have to fear: that's a basic quality of a lion. Roaring. Lions are tamable, albeit not without much effort. Lion taming requires certain characteristics. First and foremost you don't, for one moment, turn your back on the lion. If you are in the business of lion taming, you are aware the lions will challenge you. My family and I watched a young man put his trained lions through a very fascinating performance. Quite a few bandages covered his arms, eliciting our speculation. The announcer explained to the inquisitive audience that the tamer had recently experienced a mishap and was violently attacked by one of the lions. Though severely wounded, the tamer was back in the arena that same day. His courage wowed some of us, though I imagine some viewed it as stupidity. The announcer explained it was neither courage nor stupidity; rather, it was of necessity. The lion tamer had to prove to the lions he was still in control. If he stayed out of the ring too long, one of the lions would win supremacy among the pack. When the tamer returned he would find a group of lions obeying the new lion king. The new leader would be especially challenging and aggressive toward the tamer. The tamer needed to get back into the ring before this happened.

In a sense the analogy of lion taming is true regarding temptation. If you haven't been attacked, you will be. You're not defeated,

4

even though wounded by the beast of temptation, so long as you don't abandon your position. If you're down, get up, grab a whip, clutch a chair, look your enemy square in the face, and stand your ground. He is tamable!

Before I begin sounding like a sanguine spiritual guru, let me explain that this book is not a quick three steps to triumph, but it is more like a manual for combat strategy. There is no easy way with temptation. We can't pacify its devouring rage. We dare not underestimate its far-reaching talons. Unfortunately, our old nature assists this antagonist of our soul. Our flesh subtly aligns itself with the enemy and resists the Holy Spirit; our carnal nature and the Spirit are reciprocally antagonistic to each other. We dare not make compromises or peace agreements with this adversary. We must be aware, equipped, and ready for all-out war if we are to defeat the tempter. Don't become discouraged at the challenge to battle. Actually, Satan is already defeated, but he continues to skirmish with God's children on his way to his appointed eternal judgment. You and I dare not become a post-war casualty. We're on the winning team.

Points of Discussion

Discuss the lion's roar in comparison to his bite.

Why can some of the "minor temptations" be dangerous?

Discuss the danger of facing Satan with sincerity as our only defense.

Why is it important we don't spend excessive time pampering our wounds?

CHAPTER 2

Weighing the Odds

M asada was a natural fortress. Its impregnable walls defied any enemy who would dare to attack it. A handful of men could defend against many the narrow, snaking access up the eastern slope. Yet the Roman Tenth Legion, commanded by the governor of Palestine, Flavius Silva, captured Masada by attaching from the unlikely western rim. Looking out over the western wall of Masada, one wonders how anyone could hope to ascend the precipitous, rocky mountainside. Its Jewish defenders probably considered the task impossible, which could be the reason they holed up in this citadel instead of fleeing the advancing Roman army. As a tour guide related to us the story of the conquest of Masada, one of his comments was particularly intriguing. "What was that one area of vulnerability," he asked, "that permitted the Roman army to penetrate this fortress and overrun its Jewish inhabitants?"

The Romans faced formidable obstacles. Sheer cliffs protected the community atop Masada, especially the western wall. Climate offered the occupants of the mount additional protection. This area often reaches 135 degrees Fahrenheit. The Judean sun must have scorched the armor-clad Romans on the desert floor. In contrast, the Jewish Zealots occupying Masada thirteen hundred feet above them thrived in the cool breezes from the Mediterranean Sea. The Jews also enjoyed the luxury of ample water stored in huge cisterns hewn out of the mountainside. The Romans had to arduously transport water over thirty miles of rough terrain and then ration it. Yet Masada fell. How? Where was the weakness in the Jewish defense?

Flavius found the weakness. One theory says the Jewish Zealots occupying Masada refused to kill their own people (This theory is challenged by some, believing these Jews were the Sicarii, the dagger wielding assassins.), so Flavius mobilized a working force of Jewish slaves and compelled them to carry out the torturous task of building a ramp up the western slope, an unlikely ascent. Whether this theory is true or not, historical accounts and archaeological evidence show the Romans completed this massive undertaking and hauled a giant battering ram up the ramp to the western wall. They torched and breached a wooden wall (probably the weakness of Masada) atop the compound. The stories vary, but the outcome is unquestionable: the Romans conquered Masada. Perhaps the biggest mistake of the occupants was their lack of a battle strategy: they assumed the walls were ample protection to keep the enemy out. They planned no escape route. We'll talk about that more in chapter eight.

Masada can serve as a reminder that within each of us there is an area of vulnerability. Satan's strategy is to discover that particular weakness and then bombard it continually. He seeks to break down the resisting walls of our will until surrender seems inevitable. This process is temptation. The examples are endless.

> A desperate nineteen-year-old girl came for counseling. She had already been married four years and, although a child herself, was the mother of a four-year-old son. The thrill of youthful love dwindled shortly into the marriage. Her young husband was likewise experiencing adjustment problems, and the bottle had become his crutch. His immaturity prevented him from realizing the physical and emotional needs of his teenage wife. Through tears she hesitantly relayed her struggles and frustrations. On the

8

job a man was giving her the attention she needed and wanted from her husband. At first she ignored him, relying upon her commitment of marriage, but as time passed she acquiesced to his advances and flattery. The trap was baited. Although unhappily married, she sought to retain fidelity, yet she could not deny the turmoil raging within her. Initially, guilt served as a defense, helping her to rebuff the suitor's advances, but the guilt eventually became a detriment. It became a barrier to her relationship with Christ, shutting down her prayer life and leaving her more vulnerable. Feeling alienated from Christ she found it difficult to reject the intimate advances of this man. The rest is history with a sad ending.

Once a person becomes a Christian, why does he or she still battle temptations? Doesn't salvation preclude satanic advantages? Shouldn't the indwelling Holy Spirit impede impetuous decisions? Doesn't the Bible guide one around the perilous precipices and the deceptive traps set by our adversary? Since Adam and Eve were no match for the subtlety of Satan and fell prey to his devices, is it possible for us to overcome? Or like Masada, if the adversary targets us for temptation, is it inevitable that we will eventually be defeated? A prayerful and diligent study of the Word of God gives definitive answers to these questions. The Bible clearly teaches principles that, when understood and obeyed, enable Christians to be overcomers. It is hoped that this book will aid the reader in that understanding, that it will encourage someone who has previously failed to have new faith, and that it will better equip the believer for victorious living. Overcoming temptation is not always easy, but it is always possible.

If we follow biblical guidelines, victory is certain. The devil, who wants us to believe differently, perpetuates two lies to deceive us. First, he may try to convince us that overcoming is extremely easy. Anyone who believes this will be caught off guard by the intensity of his attack. Alternatively, Satan may try to convince us that it is impossible for us to overcome. Consequently, he hopes at the sound of battle—the moment of temptation—that we throw down our weapons and wave the white flag of truce. A truce is one of Satan's ploys, which will be permeated with lies. It is for this reason that we must never make a truce with Satan, for such offers opportunity for his deceptiveness. Further, Satan never honors a truce. At best it is merely a momentary reprieve in a maneuver of Satan for the ultimate destruction of the believer. A truce with Satan is a giant step toward total surrender to Satan.

Each person is unique. Everyone contends with his or her own set of weaknesses. Some weaknesses are innate, while others are acquired through a person's environment. Some people lack self-confidence, doubting their abilities or God's willingness to assist them. Others rely too much on their own strength or advantages, as perhaps was the case of the Jewish Zealots at Masada. No matter how strong we feel, we must beware lest we fall. Since Satan seems to be an expert at analyzing human character, we must be prepared at all times for his attacks by relying upon the Scripture for directive. This keeps our confidence where it should be: in God's strength.

The account of Judas Iscariot is a notable example of Satan's deceptive power and ultimate mockery of the vanquished. His weakness was greed. Deceived by Satan, he gave up his place of respect and significance in Christ's kingdom. His reward was a small sack of coins. After betraying the Lord, he became aware of the consequences of his actions, both for himself and for Christ. Overcome with remorse he returned the thirty pieces of silver to the priests. The magnitude of his sin overwhelmed him. The devil probably said something like, "You're a thief, a filthy traitor, and you don't deserve to live. You've always been a thief, and you'll never be any different." I imagine the very things Satan tempted Judas into doing in the past were the accusations that he hurled back into his face. Evidently, Judas felt no hope of change or forgiveness, and in despair he hanged himself outside the city. If Judas had repented, Jesus would have forgiven him, for Jesus forgives the vilest of sinners. Moreover, with Christ's help, Judas could have overcome his greed. No matter how hopeless a person may feel at a given time, if he repents, God will forgive him and enable him to overcome sin.

Satan used another method of attack to snare an over-confident Peter, who thought he was strong enough to remain loyal by his own determination. After professing he would never deny Jesus, even unto death, Peter denied the Lord three times by the next morning.

Like Judas, Peter experienced extreme regret for his failure. Unlike Judas, he sought forgiveness, found Christ to be full of compassion, and learned from his mistake. He accepted his human frailty but learned to rely on the power of the Holy Spirit rather than his own abilities. Consequently, we find Peter preaching the keynote sermon on the Day of Pentecost and carrying the message of the Gospel to the Jewish, Samaritan, and Gentile communities. Many people try to overcome temptation by their own strength, and as a result they live with failure and guilt. Victory is attainable, not by the strength of the human will or intellect, but by the overcoming power of God that indwells the believer. The Bible says, "Not by might, nor by power, but by my spirit, saith the Lord of hosts" (Zechariah 4:6). Scripture doesn't indicate overcoming sin is easy, but it does teach it is absolutely possible. All twenty-one epistles were written to exhort the believer to overcome sin. Paul sheds insight to the constant battle when he expressed, "...I die daily" (I Corinthians 15:31). Every day had its struggles. Peter warned that the devil "...as a roaring lion, walketh about, seeking whom he may devour" (I Peter 5:8). John spoke of a loving Savior, who would forgive us our sins if we asked, but he also admonished us to refrain from sin (I John 2:1). Paul encouraged, "There hath no temptation taken you but such as is common to man: but God is faithful, who will not suffer you to be tempted above that ye are able; but will with the temptation also make a way to escape, that ye may be able to bear it" (I Corinthians 10:13). Paul recalled the time in Damascus when evil men waited at every gate to capture him. But the brethren helped Paul escape by lowering him over the city wall in a basket. There had been a way out of the imminent danger facing him. If God could help him to evade the enemy in Damascus, then He could provide a way to elude sin in the midst of temptation. There will always be a rope, a basket, a window, a door—always a way of escape from sin. To the Philippian church, which questioned the sensibility of his imprisonment, Paul encouraged, "I can do all things through Christ which strengtheneth me" (Philippians 4:13). From his prison cell Paul wrote that with God's power we can always be stronger than trials, temptations, sin, and Satan.

Sometimes we confuse temptation with sin, but the two are vastly different. Because we are mortals, have the devil as an enemy, and live in a sinful world, we certainly will have temptations. But the temptation itself is not sin. Sin begins when we surrender to the temptation by following carnal desires to the place of committing acts or by purposefully entertaining thoughts contrary to God's morality. Sin has not always existed in the human race. God created Adam and Eve as perfect beings; sin was not an innate part of their nature. God created man in His own likeness: a likeness that included moral purity. Adam's language was completely free from profanity or blasphemy. He spoke only the beautiful language the Lord had given him. No sinful thought or evil desire polluted his mind. Lying was unknown to him. Adam and Eve were sinless. Satan introduced the only sin Adam and Eve could commit, the sin of disobedience. The Lord had given only one negative commandment to Adam and Eve: "Of the tree of the knowledge of good and evil, thou shalt not eat of it" (Genesis 2:17). As long as they obeyed this singular command, they had no desire to commit other sins. Obedience was the only command God gave them, and in reality, it is our only command today.

With sin being completely foreign to Adam and Eve, how then did they sin? God did not create Adam and Eve as robots. God created them with a free will; they could choose to do as they pleased. He gave them a choice to obey or to disobey Him. Since they knew no sin to commit and had no desire to commit sin, they were without temptation. The utopia in the garden was interrupted when Satan introduced temptation. Like as Adam and Eve, neither are we robots today. As Adam and Eve experienced freedom of choice, we are likewise privileged to make choices. In contrast to Adam and Eve before their fall, we are the recipients of their fallen nature. Even without Satan to tempt us, we would still experience temptation from our human, innate nature. Our temptation is twofold: Satanic temptation and innate human desires.

Why would God allow Satan to tempt Adam and Eve? Temptation was about choices. Temptation is still about choices. Why does God allow us to be tempted? I can't speak for God, but I think from the general knowledge of His Word, our unique design—with a free will, which we would never want to relinquish—makes us God's preeminent creation. God receives no pleasure in our struggle against sin. God, who has manifested His kindness from the dawn of creation, desires the best for His people. Adam and Eve didn't have to fail. God gave them many trees from which to eat, and all of them were "pleasant to the sight, and good for food" (Genesis 2:9). Among these trees were the tree of life and the tree of the knowledge of good and evil. Both the tree of good and evil and the tree of life were accessible (otherwise, man wouldn't have had the freedom of choice), but God commanded Adam and Eve not to eat of the tree of the knowledge of good and evil. Satan tempted them to disobey this command by lying to them about God's motives. This is an example of Satan using partial truth. If they had eaten from the tree of life, they may well have become unique like God: eternal (Genesis 3:22), but Satan focused on the tree of good and evil and tempted them to partake. Instead of eating from the tree of life, they ate from the tree suggested by Satan. They chose the forbidden tree and thus lost their access to the tree of life. By eating the forbidden fruit, as God warned, they became sinners (spiritual death), the clock of mortality started ticking (physical death), and the curse was passed to all future mankind.

In the midst of a fallen creation, we still see the beauty of nature surrounding us today. It is a testimony of the intent of God for His creation. More than natural beauty, God has made available to mankind some wonderfully and spiritually fulfilling experiences. As in the Garden of Eden, however, He still has certain guidelines for us to follow—not to deny us pleasure—in order for us to remain undefiled by the world and to experience His ultimate joy, peace, and contentment. When man does not control his sinful desires, he stumbles blindly down a path of unrest, discontent, and insatiable lusts. One abuse leads to another. Man searches, but he cannot find the key to happiness in his own realm. Only in the grace of God that comes through Jesus Christ can a person find restoration to joy and contentment.

We're not certain how long the temptation lasted, whether it was a one-time temptation or over a period of visits. We are aware Satan concealed his identity as a fallen angel by appearing as a serpent. The Bible describes the serpent as the subtlest beast God had created. The Hebrew word for subtle alludes to the serpent's cunningness, and it suggests the serpent was such a common sight in the garden that his presence caused no undue alarm. Eve wasn't startled or frightened away at his presence, so it appears Satan chose a familiar form in which to encounter her. Throughout Scripture, a prominent characteristic of Satan is deceitfulness. He takes on a form that man accepts. Paul described him as "transformed into an angel of light" (II Corinthians 11:14). The Greek word *mĕtaschēmatizō,* translated transform, means to "disguise or transfigure."[3] It is to disguise the inner nature by camouflaging the outward man. Satan hid his true nature in the garden by manifesting himself as a serpent. This snake was unusual compared to our understanding of snakes. The snake walked upright. Before you write me off as a simpleton, consider this discovery reported by National Geographic. "Snakes slithered onto the scene…when dinosaurs still roamed the earth. More primitive snakes such as boas and pythons have traces of hind leg bones in their skeleton…."[4] Cartoonists make light of the Bible story: a little snake is coiled around a branch watching Adam and Eve share an apple. When we consider the real picture, we can envision a twenty-feet tall boa waltzing through the garden. Eve, awed by his dinosaur-like features, is even more captivated when he strikes up a conversation. He deceives her with his subtlety. Adam and Eve lost their favored status with God. The serpent lost his charm. Someone humorously expressed, Satan walked into the garden, but he crawled out. God cursed the serpent and caused it to crawl in the dust of the ground as a reminder of his association with the fallen angel, Satan. The prophets describe Satan's fall from heaven in a similar manner: "How art thou cut down to the ground" (Isaiah 14:12); "I will cast thee to the ground" (Ezekiel 28:17).

Satan has established the earth as his base. He proclaims himself to be the prince of this world and guards his kingdom against the Lord. God has no problem in recapturing the earth from Satan; His power over Satan is absolute. The true area of struggle is in redeeming willful, wayward mankind without destroying His creation. Through Calvary God provided redemption for mankind, but as in the Garden of Eden He still gives man the choice to accept or reject salvation. God did not force Adam and Eve to eat from the tree of life, nor does He force mankind today to drink from the fountain of life: Christ. The choice still belongs to mankind. By the disobedience of one man—Adam—all were made sinners. By the obedience of one man—Christ—all can be made righteous (Romans 5:19). God stands ready to aid us in our battle to overcome. His ability to assist us is infinite, so without question we can be successful in our struggle. To realize the magnitude of God's power, we need only look at the grandeur of creation, and even this reveals but a small fraction of God's power. The earth is part of a galaxy called the Milky Way. From tip to tip this galaxy spans a distance of over five quintillion miles (unfathomable by human standards). It contains over thirty billion suns, and our sun alone is one and a half million times larger than the earth. Moreover, our galaxy is only one of more than one hundred billion in the observable universe, and the universe extends far into the unobservable. These statistics are based only upon man's present limited knowledge of the universe. Creation thus reveals the power and splendor of God. By contrast, man is small and insignificant. Yet man meant so much to God that of all the one hundred billion galaxies and all the planets in the galaxies, He focused upon the earth, manifested Himself in flesh, and as the Son of God gave His human life to purchase our salvation. We cannot fathom God's love, but His Word states, "I will never leave thee, nor forsake thee" (Hebrews 13:5).

If Satan can't convince you against the fallen nature of mankind, that there is no right or wrong, he will try and convince you there is no removal of your sin. Guilt and hopelessness become the substitute stumbling block. We'll tackle this subject in a subsequent chapter. For now, suffice it to quote Paul, "For whosoever shall call upon the name of the Lord shall be saved" (Romans 10:13).

The adversary breached Masada's supposedly impregnable walls. The fortress' purpose failed because Masada represented man's ingenuity, and the more powerful, resourceful, and experienced won the battle. Though deeply religious and extremely courageous, the zealots inhabiting Masada fought for an earthly cause, though they probably construed it as a heavenly cause. Our battle is spiritual, Paul explained to the Ephesian believers; therefore, it is not won through traditional warfare. "For we wrestle not against flesh and blood, but against principalities, against powers, against the rulers of the darkness of this world, against spiritual wickedness in high places" (Ephesians 6:12). First and foremost the battle Satan wages against us is also against the Lord. That makes the odds uniquely different and the outcome sure. Victory is promised. God cannot lie. He's never lost a battle. Further, by way of Calvary, He has proven His intentions regarding our future. He planned our salvation. He purchased our salvation. He desires us to be saved. He wants us to lead a joyful, victorious life. He intends for us to overcome temptation. We're not destined to become a Masada statistic; we are destined for victory over temptation.

Points of Discussion

How do we identify personal vulnerabilities?

Once we identify an area of vulnerability, what precautions should we establish in our lives to prevent falling into sin?

What weaknesses might Judas have neglected that contributed to his betrayal of Christ?

Discuss the difference between temptation and sin.

CHAPTER 3

Knowing Our Enemy

S atan has lied to us about his power. To plan an effective defense
strategy, we must know the truth about our enemy. He's convinced us our best-case scenario is to leave our borders of defense
and hunker down twenty miles inside our safe zone. We're somewhat persuaded there's exemption from all-out war if we keep our
head down and make few waves. The truth is, whether we fight on
his territory or on our own, Satan is at war against us. Our best defense is a good offense, and in order to keep Satan at bay, we need to
be knowledgeable about his background and his past tactics.

Let's be reasonable. In a real war, where is the safe zone for a
country? Is it having the defensive line drawn twenty miles inside
our borders? Is it logical and safe for our family and friends to allow
the enemy to advance inside our lives before we create a defensive
maneuver? Isn't it safer to have a border, buffeted by a neutral zone,
where the enemy isn't allowed to enter? This is more realistic but
still inadequate. We need background information on the operations
of Satan. Further, we need to recognize Satan is our enemy even
before he attacks. We need to understand his history of aggression.

This enables us to have both an offensive and defensive battle strategy in place at all times. We can collect an astounding amount of information about his tactics by studying the Scripture.

We have little information regarding Satan in the eons past, but this in no way gives him an edge. Our Commander-in-Chief created and controls his very existence. Though the Bible may be silent regarding certain information about Satan, such silence doesn't mean our omniscient God is unaware. As an analogy, the bank president doesn't call every customer when one individual overdraws his bank account. Neither does God reveal all His actions in maintaining universal order past and present, especially in dealing with Satan. The Bible is almost silent regarding pre-creation history. Of the bits and pieces of information scattered throughout the Scripture, we arrive at some conclusions. In his original state, Satan was perfect, for God never has created and never will create anything evil. Still, God allows for a certain amount of choice in His creation, with consequences. Though a leading angel in heaven, Satan fell from his created position because of self-exaltation. See Isaiah 14:12-15 and Ezekiel 28:11-19 for the descriptive imagery of Satan's demotion in the angelic rank of heaven. Delighting in the God-created magnificence of his person, over time, Satan developed a prideful stance regarding his significance. He left his post as the worship leader and desired others worship him. He lost purpose in reflecting the glory of God and wanted to be equal with God. His prideful choice assumed he could perform as God's counterpart or even assumed he could acquire a position above the Creator. His inner desires became so apparent that an open confrontation resulted, and the heavens blazed with celestial warfare. Satan lost! How shall we describe the war? How about a single gnat attacking an elephant? No, that's too extreme. A single gnat attacking a herd of elephants would be a better analogy. I think you get the picture. God ordered Satan and his angelic cronies out of heaven. This vast multitude of evil spirits took up residence and eventually possessed seats of authority on earth. Still full of self, Satan organized these fallen cherubs into a spiritual army with rank and order, commissioned by him to attack, conquer, and harass God's creation.

By order of creation, mankind is lower than the angels in the scale of authority. The Bible declares, "But one in a certain place testified, saying, What is man, that thou art mindful of him? or the son of man that thou visitest him? Thou madest him a little lower than the angels; thou crownedst him with glory and honour, and didst set him over the works of thy hands" (Hebrews 2:6-7). Since we're subordinate in authority to Satan and the angels allied with him, it's necessary for us to identify with Christ and rely upon His authority to combat Satan's kingdom. An analogy could be an individual being attacked by a giant corporation attempting to acquire their property by force, manipulation, or at a substantially reduced value. The individual is no match for the resources and power wielded by a giant conglomerate, and the individual is sure to loose. The individual's only recourse is to appeal to a higher authority than the corporation: the legal system to which both the individual and the giant corporation must acquiesce. Humans, even earthly empires, are no match for, and have succumbed to, Satan's influence. Paul wrote regarding the severity of this spiritual warfare, "Put on the whole armour of God, that ye may be able to stand against the wiles of the devil. For we wrestle not against flesh and blood, but against principalities, against powers, against the rulers of the darkness of this world, against spiritual wickedness in high places" (Ephesians 6:11-12).

One piece of armor necessary for our protection against Satan is truth (Ephesians 6:14). In order to live an overcoming life, we must be knowledgeable of what the Bible says about our adversary. There are two important truths we need to understand and stand upon. One, Satan's power is great. He is ruthless and lethal to the ill-equipped. Satan is very real and has an element of authority over mankind. He reigns over an organized spirit kingdom far more powerful than any kingdom established by man.

The second truth we must understand is Satan's power is limited: he must submit to God's authority. True, Satan is powerful, but unlike God, he is not all-powerful. To the contrary, Satan's power originally came from God, is continually derived from God, and is always subject to God. Satan is a created being; he is not a creator. Satan can exercise power only as far as God permits and only as long as God permits.

The creation (angels, humankind, and the animal kingdom) must operate according to the order of authority established by the only Creator: the God of Scripture. Since God created mankind a little lower than the angels, we are in subjection to their authority. As the abilities of the animal kingdom are inferior to that of mankind, so man's abilities are below those of the angelic host, including both good and evil angels. Angels are capable of feats impossible for man. While man can build space vehicles that travel at the speed of a bullet, angels can appear and disappear at will, perhaps traveling at the speed of thought. This doesn't mean we are at the mercy of evil spirits. Even though the evil spirits rebelled against God, they are still subject to His ultimate authority. Jesus, who was literally God robed in humanity, encountered numerous cases of demon possession during His earthly ministry. Not once was He defeated, and He showed Himself master over the demonic world as time and again the evil spirits were subject to Him. At one such confrontation, the demons asked Christ, "Art thou come hither to torment us before the time?" (Matthew 8:29). The fear of impending judgment brought the demons running to Jesus, as if He had summoned them, and they pleaded with Him to spare them immediate judgment. Jesus spared them from being cast into the lake of fire prematurely (before the end of the world) and allowed them to enter into a herd of swine. "Go" (Matthew 8:32), Jesus said. At this singular command, the evil spirits fled from His presence and entered into the swine. This incident demonstrates the limitations of satanic authority. The demons did not argue with Jesus; they simply obeyed. They entered into a herd of two thousand pigs, which, unaccustomed to demonic influence, reacted adversely to this sinister invasion and plunged from the rocky cliffs of Gergesa into the Sea of Galilee and perished. The evil spirits were permitted to bring death to the swine, but Jesus demanded they release their human captive. Though they brought much anguish to the man they possessed, they were limited in their power over the man. They could dwell in him and torment him, but they could not kill him, for the power over life and death is not indiscriminately granted unto the demon world. Demons cannot do anything to man that God does not allow. To attempt to do so would place them in danger of premature punishment. If we request God's intervention against Satan's attacks, then Satan must retreat. This is a Biblical principle.

The book of Job shares the ultimate attack of Satan against an individual. Through this account we readily see, though Satan pushed Job to the limit, God established the parameters by which Satan could attack. At first, Satan accused Job of self-interest, that he served God only to acquire God's hedge of protection. Satan was partially correct in his observation, for God did have a defense surrounding Job, but Satan was wrong in his assumptions regarding Job's motives of living for God. The hedge was a blessing God bestowed upon Job because of Job's fear of the Lord, love for righteousness, and hatred of evil. Likewise, the Apostle Peter described those who serve Christ as "a peculiar people" (I Peter 2:9). Some of the meaning of this phrase is lost in translation. Kenneth Wuest describes the Greek word translated "peculiar" more specifically: "a dot being surrounded by a circle."[5] In this descriptive language, we are the dot, and God is the circle. As God's people we are encircled by His presence. We are peculiar, not in a sense of odd or strange, but in a sense of our position and favor with God. We are unique from those who don't live for God in that His protection surrounds us continuously. Further, Satan cannot penetrate God's line of defense unless allowed by the Lord. With such keen insight regarding spiritual warfare, Paul wrote to the Corinthian church, "There hath no temptation taken you but such as is common to man: but God is faithful, who will not suffer you to be tempted above that ye are able; but will with the temptation also make a way to escape, that ye may be able to bear it" (I Corinthians 10:13). Mr. Wuest also offers an explanation for this Scripture. "The Greek word translated "temptation" has two meanings, first, "a time of testing or trial," second, "a solicitation to do evil."[6] He clarifies, God both allows, even sometimes plans the test, but He always limits the extent of temptation. He allows temptation for some higher purpose of which we aren't always aware; he limits temptation for our purpose, that we may not be overwhelmed by Satan. We see these two principles at work in the story of Job. In order to demonstrate Job's reliance upon Him, God permitted Satan to penetrate the hedge. At the same time God placed limitations upon Satan. Satan could hurt the things that belonged to Job, but he could not touch Job. Later, God allowed Satan to afflict Job's body, but he still could not take Job's life. God allowed Job's temptation, but He limited what Satan could do to him. In all this, Job remained faithful to the Lord.

Some are quick to point out the terrible things that happened to Job are little consolation to us regarding God's protective hedge. Please note that Job was God's example of the ages. God never again needs to duplicate this scenario between Himself and Satan. Mankind's ability to love God in spite of the circumstances was proven to Satan. Our focus regarding Job's example should be that God is in charge. He is the referee: He stands in the ring, not only to assure our victory, but if need be, to take the punches for us. As God limited Satan in what he could do to Job, He limits him in what he can do to us. Our task is to maintain our trust in God's provision and continue our commitment to Him: trust and obey. There is a limit to every temptation: both a time limit and the degree of severity of the trial that Satan may apply against us. Satan has assumed much. Since his original sin was self-exaltation, it's no marvel he assumed titles and roles not rightly his. He's like a condemned criminal on death row that talks as if he controls organized crime on the streets. He claims ownership of the world and makes promises accordingly. Satan made absurd promises when tempting Christ. "And the devil, taking him up into an high mountain, shewed unto him all the kingdoms of the world in a moment of time. And the devil said unto him, All this power will I give thee, and the glory of them: for that is delivered unto me; and to whomsoever I will I give it. If thou therefore wilt worship me, all shall be thine" (Luke 4:5-7). In actuality, Satan owns nothing. "The earth is the LORD's, and the fulness thereof; the world, and they that dwell therein" (Psalms 24:1). He is the "prince of this world" (John 12:31; 14:30; 16:11) and the "god of this world" (II Corinthians 4:4) only by reason that mankind submits to his rule. Satan is the tempter, the adversary, and the accuser of the brethren (Matthew 4:3; I Thessalonians 3:5; I Peter 5:8; Revelation 12:10) only because Adam and Eve succumbed to his voice in the Garden and lost the safe-haven of God's continual fellowship. At the final judgment God will dismiss Satan of titles and roles, terminate his authority, and confine him to eternal captivity and punishment. In the meantime Satan is powerless except for the created authority God allows him to exercise. We are assured God will not allow the devil to tempt us beyond our capacity to bear it (I Corinthians 10:13).

Still, after considering the Biblical clarification regarding Satan's limited power, it is imperative we remain unpresumptuous in our Christian walk, living as if Satan is at our command. We must realize that human power is inferior to that of angels (God has not yet rescinded the power of evil angels). Even the archangel Michael—a principal angel of God but subordinate to Lucifer by way of the creation—did not personally rebuke Satan. He stated, "The Lord rebuke thee" (Jude 9). This example vividly displays the creative chain of authority. The angel Michael didn't consider himself of equal power with Satan but realized his control over Satan was through the Lord's authority. We are insufficient within ourselves to overcome Satan. Through Christ, however, we are "more than conquerors" (Romans 8:37). We can do all things through Christ, and this includes overcoming Satan. The common expression, "Give the devil a black eye," and the child's song, "The devil is a sly old fox, if I could catch him I'd put him in a box" are sincere but misleading. Within ourselves we are powerless against Satan, but through God's power we are victorious. We should remain unpresumptuous, but we should not be fearful. The Bible admonishes, "Fear not, little flock; for it is your Father's good pleasure to give you the kingdom" (Luke 12:32). Someone calculated the Bible tells us more than three hundred and sixty-five times to not be afraid. That's once for every day of the year. Paul wrote, "Be careful for nothing; but in every thing by prayer and supplication with thanksgiving let your requests be made known unto God." (Philippians 4:6). Paul literally said, "Don't worry about anything." He told us what not to do, but also gave us two directives on what we should do: pray earnestly about everything and be thankful to God for His provision. We should not be filled with anxiety about Satan and what he might do to us; in contrast, we should express our concerns through prayer and acknowledge our thanks through praise. Paul painted a word picture of the final scene in his writing to the Christians in Rome, "God...shall bruise Satan under your feet shortly" (Romans 16:20).

God uses a praying church to thwart the devil's schemes. The church is a spiritual entity, and its battles mustn't be viewed and gaged according to human standards. Even when the devil seemingly wins a battle against a Christian, the Lord turns that apparent defeat into victory. John wrote, "Fear none of those things which thou shalt suffer; behold, the devil shall cast some of you into prison, that ye may be tried…be thou faithful unto death, and I will give thee a crown of life" (Revelation 2:10). Notice the text indicates death is not the end; death is the door through which the tempted person passes into victory. Death for the non-believer is the door to damnation, but for the Christian it is the Arch of Triumph. Paul redefined death for the believer. He considered death to be "gain" for a Christian (Philippians 1:21). Satan may well hesitate to kill a saint, even if God would permit it, for this would automatically insure the believer an eternal "crown of life."

We live in a stressful society. Jesus said that in the last days there would come "distress of nations, with perplexity…men's hearts failing them for fear" (Luke 21:15-26). Doctor John T. Biggs, a St. Louis physician, stressed (no pun intended), "Stress is implicated in fifty percent of all patient-doctor visits."[7] Likewise, doctors acknowledge that fear contributes directly to multiple diseases. The child of God need not fall prey to one of these stress-related diseases. Satan wants to destroy us by getting us to "bear tomorrow's problems with only today's grace." He discourages us with yesterday's failures and stops our progress by tomorrow's fears. We must learn to live one day at a time, relying upon Christ's promise, "My grace is sufficient" (II Corinthians 12:9) and by praying according to Christ's model prayer, "Give us this day our daily bread" (Matthew 6:11).

Though the Bible indicates Satan dominates fallen mankind, let us recognize the Incarnation reversed our state with God "For ye are all the children of God by faith in Christ Jesus" (Galatians 3:8). The Bible proclaims Christ has "all power in heaven and in earth" (Matthew 28:18). Satan assumes a seat with temporary authority. Because of Calvary, Satan is but a figurehead, for from the foundation of the world, God set in motion a plan that terminates his authority. In contrast to the Garden scene, where Lucifer dominated and decimated mankind through the subtlety of the serpent, Christ has universal control, and His overcoming power is resident within us "Ye are of God, little children, and have overcome them: because greater is he that is in you, than he that is in the world. (I John 4:4).

Due to the chain of events since creation, the devil's primary weapon is deception. The Gospel writer, John, describes Satan: "…he is a liar, and the father of it" (8:44). The devil is the inventor of the lie. One lie that Satan projects is his claim to be God. During the Great Tribulation, Satan will set himself up as God on the earth, and men will worship him (II Thessalonians 2:4). Even today, Satan deceives many by his lies. In particular, Satan lays claim to attributes that belong to God alone. God is omnipotent (all-powerful), omniscient (all-knowing), and omnipresent (everywhere present). Satan wants us to believe he possesses these attributes also, but he does not. He has no power except what God allows. Though Satan's influence is universal, he cannot be everywhere at the same time. There are certain things of which God alone is cognizant. Satan may project thoughts onto us by way of our sinful and frail nature, and he can assume what we are thinking by reason of our demeanor, but he doesn't necessarily know our thoughts and cannot control our reasoning. His power is limited and will eventually be withdrawn.

Some mistakenly assume the devil will reign over the wicked and torment them in the lake of fire. Paintings portray the devil as the ruler over hell, sitting on a fiery throne holding a pitchfork for a scepter. Not so. The devil, as an insubordinate created being, will be ceremoniously stripped of his rank and authority. The lake of fire will be as torturous for him as for anyone else. Like a cowering criminal condemned to death, he will crawl and beg before the judgment throne of God. In the sight of all mankind, God will cast him into the lake of fire, to receive eternal punishment. The prophet Isaiah penned this description of Satan's future:

> Thou shalt be brought down to hell, to the sides of the pit. They that see thee shall narrowly look upon thee, and consider thee, saying, "Is this the man that made the earth to tremble, that did shake kingdoms; that made the world as a wilderness, and destroyed the cities thereof; that opened not the house of his prisoners."
>
> Isaiah 14:15-17

What a humiliation Satan will receive when God reduces him lower than mankind! His future is set, and he cannot alter it. He continues his prideful operation as if he is God. Satan knows only those things God innately allowed, or he learned since creation. His knowledge is limited. He is a good guesser, and he knows much about human nature, but he does not know everything. Neither is the devil everywhere, although he moves about from place to place. He can be either here or there, but he cannot he here and there at the same time. He dispatches demons to various places and makes his influence felt everywhere, but he is limited to one place at a time. Only God is all-powerful, all-knowing, and everywhere present. Satan is limited.

Here's the good news. The church will outlast the devil: "And I say also unto thee, That thou art Peter, and upon this rock I will build my church; and the gates of hell shall not prevail against it" (Matthew 16:18). The Book of Revelation reveals Satan's eternal defeat. The lion will be caged. Chapters twenty-one and twenty-two of the Book of Revelation show us the church's eternal victory—the bride of Christ's triumphant appearance. The Bible is positive about this spiritual warfare. The church will win. It's guaranteed by Calvary.

Points of Discussion

How could Lucifer, so perfect in his original state of creation, become so evil?

Discuss humankind's subordination to angels—including the fallen angels.

Since we are no match for Satan's power, how can we overcome his attacks?

Compare the attributes of God (omnipotent, omnipresent, omniscient) with those of Satan.

CHAPTER 4

God's Plan of Redemption

Calvary! It is a love story unequaled. Man's imagination could not conceive of a plan more perfect in love. The Creator of the universe became the Savior of His creation. Man's fall in the Garden of Eden had two adverse consequences. First, he acquired a sinful, fallen nature he cannot eradicate. All of mankind received this sinful nature from Adam through inheritance (Romans 3:9; 5:12, 19), his spiritual qualities died, and his physical qualities became subject to death: he became carnal and mortal in a moment's time. As David confessed, "Behold, I was shapen in iniquity; and in sin did my mother conceive me" (Psalm 51:5), so it is true for all mankind. The sinful nature compels man to sin, and the unregenerate man has no power to stop sinning. He may not repeat Cain's sin and become a murderer, but he commits murder in his heart because he has the same nature as Cain.

Second, sinful man lost fellowship with God. God and sin are incompatible, so man's sin separated him from God. Rather than destroy His creation, God withdrew. Thus, man needs both a regeneration of heart and restoration to fellowship with God. One without the other is inadequate and, indeed, impossible. Since man could accomplish neither by his own power, man's salvation required divine intervention.

God took the initiative in restoring fellowship with fallen man by allowing an animal sacrifice to atone or compensate for mankind's sins. Man's sinful nature remained a problem. Simply reinstating man into God's fellowship didn't solve this problem, for man was controlled by the sinful nature. Mankind was trapped in a vicious cycle of sin, sacrifice, sin, sacrifice. The Mosaic Law brought a measure of change due to the disciplinary actions upon the offender, but the Law failed in that it didn't change the heart. Just as a cat chases mice because it is a cat, so man sins because he is a sinner. God had to design a plan both to reinstate man into His fellowship and to conquer man's fallen nature. Calvary was God's solution. Christ became the perfect sacrifice. He who never sinned was judged as a sinner, and His sacrificial death was ample payment for mankind's accumulated debt of sin. Further, the New Birth experience gave mankind new and godly desires, and the Holy Spirit equipped him to combat the old nature inherited from Adam.

Calvary was not an afterthought. The Bible declares Christ to be "the Lamb slain from the foundation of the world" (Revelation 13:8). God foreordained Calvary before He created the world. Does this mean God predestined each individual to be saved or lost? No, it was an equal opportunity plan. An individual's salvation rests in his personal acceptance of God's grace rather than an arbitrary choice by God to save selectively. "For God so loved the world, that he gave his only begotten Son, that whosoever believeth in him should not perish, but have everlasting life" (John 3:16). (See also II Peter 3:9; Revelation 22:17.)

God foreordained the plan of salvation because in His foreknowledge He saw that Adam and Eve would yield to Satan's temptation. If God foreknew this, why did He proceed with creation? He created man in love, knowing that although man would fail, there would be a plan of redemption for him. God's plan was to manifest Himself in flesh. As a man He would be born into the world, dwell with man, suffer all that man suffers, be tempted of the devil, live a sinless life, endure the death of Calvary, and resurrect Himself from the dead. In this way He would become the substitute sacrifice for the created beings He loved so much. He would pay the ultimate price of death to buy back His creation from the clutches of death and Satan. The Scripture is clear regarding the manner in which God brought redemption: "...the church of God, which he hath purchased with his own blood" (Acts 20:28). "Neither by the blood of goats and calves, but by his own blood he entered in once into the holy place, having obtained eternal redemption for us" (Hebrews 9:12).

All of humanity has access to redemption, but all do not accept or believe Scripture. Acceptance or rejection of God's redemptive plan rests upon the shoulders of each individual. "Therefore as by the offence of one judgment came upon all men to condemnation; even so by the righteousness of one the free gift came upon all men unto justification of life. For as by one man's disobedience many were made sinners, so by the obedience of one shall many be made righteous" (Romans 5:18-19). "For as in Adam all die, even so in Christ shall all be made alive" (I Corinthians 15:22).

Man's fall was not an easy situation to reconcile. The moral attributes of God are from eternity and cannot change. These were incumbent upon the creation. When mankind sinned, the consequences were catastrophic. God's holiness demanded separation from sinful man. Sin broke communion between the Creator and His creation. Moreover, God's justice placed man under the sentence of death, both physical and spiritual, for God had warned, "The day thou eatest thereof thou shalt surely die" (Genesis 2:17). Man broke the command of God, and God's justice demanded punishment. On the other hand, the mercy of God pleaded for pardon. Justice required death while mercy sought life. The grace and love of God presented a beautiful plan that satisfied both justice and mercy. The death of the sinless Christ paid the penalty justice required, while all who accept Christ's death and apply it to their own lives receive the pardon mercy sought to provide.

The first scriptural indication of God's redemptive plan occurs in Genesis 3, the same chapter that describes man's fall. God wasted no time in proclaiming hope. To the serpent God said, "I will put enmity between thee and the woman, and between thy seed and her seed; it shall bruise thy head, and thou shalt bruise his heel" (Genesis 3:15). In retrospect, this is the first of a series of Messianic prophecies. Only after Calvary, the birth of the church, and the completion of the New Testament do these prophecies become clear. The plan of redemption became personal through the Incarnation (God became man). God became human but untainted by the sin of Adam. The New Testament declares Him as the last Adam: "And so it is written, The first man Adam was made a living soul; the last Adam was made a quickening spirit" (I Corinthians 15:45). The first Adam brought death by his actions; the last Adam brought life by His sacrificial death. Christ acquired all the moral attributes of God by reason of his conception being of deity origination. He acquired his physical characteristics (free of the inherited sin of Adam) by reason of conception through Mary. His was the only conception of deity: "...the only begotten Son of God" (John 3:18). "And the Word was made flesh, and dwelt among us, (and we beheld his glory, the glory as of the only begotten of the Father,) full of grace and truth" (John 1:14). Christ's ultimate purpose was to become the "lamb of God." He lived a sinless life and yet received the punishment of a sinner: death. He suffered a bruised heel at Calvary, but Calvary was not the end. An empty tomb followed. As the sin of one man, Adam, passed on a sinful nature to all mankind, Christ offers the New Birth to all, passing His righteousness unto whosoever will.

God established a plan in the Garden of Eden that He followed throughout the entire Bible. He demanded the shedding of blood—death—to cover sin. "Without shedding of blood is no remission" (Hebrews 9:22). Adam and Eve hid from the presence of God in the Garden; they attempted to cover their shame by sewing leaves together for a covering. Innocence vanished, and guilt replaced their virtuousness. God rejected their leafy clothing and provided them ample covering with coats of animal skins. This indicates two principles: consciousness of sin and the need of the Savior. The predetermined verdict for sin was death; the prearranged strategy for redemption required a substitutionary death. The skin of an innocent animal covered their shame (nakedness). The death of an animal stayed Adam and Eve's death penalty.

From Adam's sin to the law given on Mount Sinai, God required blood sacrifices to meet the demands of His justice. Abel, Noah, Abraham, Isaac, Jacob, and the Israelites who sacrificed the Passover lamb before fleeing Egyptian bondage all offered animal sacrifices to atone for their guilt. Prior to the Mosaic Law, the Bible records no specific directions concerning blood sacrifices, but it is clear from Biblical examples that man followed the pattern set by the Lord in Eden. Those desiring God's fellowship offered substitute sacrifices for sin. The Law of Moses gave specific instructions regarding blood sacrifices, and these were still in effect during Christ's earthly ministry. Even so, man still lived under the guilt and overwhelming power of his sinful nature. Man's dilemma needed heavenly intervention.

Throughout the Old Testament there are indications that animal sacrifices alone were insufficient to atone for man's sins. Samuel declared to Saul, "Hath the LORD as great delight in burnt offerings and sacrifices, as in obeying the voice of the LORD? Behold, to obey is better than sacrifice, and to hearken than the fat of rams" (I Samuel 15:22). The prophet Isaiah wrote, "To what purpose is the multitude of your sacrifices unto me? saith the LORD: I am full of the burnt offerings of rams, and the fat of fed beasts; and I delight not in the blood of bullocks, or of lambs, or of he goats" (Isaiah 1:11).

The writer of The Book of Hebrews explained that the Old Testament Tabernacle, replete with animal sacrifices, "was a figure for the time then present, in which were offered both gifts and sacrifices, that could not make him that did the service perfect, as pertaining to the conscience" (Hebrews 9:9). Animal sacrifices only foreshadowed Christ's death and had no power in themselves to forgive sins.

> For the law having a shadow of good things to come, and not the very image of the things, can never with those sacrifices which they offered year by year continually make the comers thereunto perfect. But in those sacrifices there is a remembrance again made of sins every year. For it is not possible that the blood of bulls and of goats should take away sins.
>
> Hebrews 10:1, 3-4).

Mount Calvary is the focal point of all history. Sins of the past, present, and future were nailed to the cross of Christ. None of the lambs slain before Calvary as a sacrifice for man's sin could actually remit sin. They simply postponed the judgment of God. Death held its prey (all mankind) captive, and the blood of a million animals could not sever the chains. Satan probably mocked the seemingly futile efforts of sinful man as he brought his prized lamb to be sacrificed.

Calvary changed everything. Christ became the perfect substitute lamb for man's sin. His death was sufficient to remove man's sin and guilt and to loose the chains of death. It is no coincidence that many graves were opened and many saints restored to life at the resurrection of Christ (Matthew 27:52-53).

The crucifixion took place almost two thousand years ago. The blood of Christ covered both past and future sins. We obtain salvation through obedient faith in Jesus Christ's atoning blood. We express our faith in Christ by obedience to His New Birth plan of salvation, and we preserve our salvation by continuance in faith. What about those who lived prior to the New Testament and had no access to Christ's atonement? God judges those who lived before Calvary according to their obedient faith in God's revelation to them, whether it was by conscience, the written Word, or the voice of the prophet. If they manifest obedient faith in God, the blood of Christ flowed backwards and covered their sins. They, too, will stand before God guiltless through Christ. The Psalmist David prophesied, "I have set the LORD always before me: because he is at my right hand, I shall not be moved. Therefore my heart is glad, and my glory rejoiceth: my flesh also shall rest in hope. For thou wilt not leave my soul in hell; neither wilt thou suffer thine Holy One to see corruption" (Psalms 16:8-10). He spoke of Christ's resurrection, which assured those of pre-Calvary a hope. His confidence was in Christ's atoning sacrifice.

There are two kinds of faith: an acknowledging faith and a saving faith. An acknowledging faith is merely a mental profession of belief in God's existence. It may even include an acknowledgment of God's saving power. All mankind can have this type of faith simply by observing God's handiwork in creation. We see the world around us and acknowledge the existence of an unseen Creator God. Acknowledging faith alone does not save us; in fact, it condemns us unless we act upon our faith in obedience to our knowledge of God and His Word.

Rejection of acknowledging faith leads one to humanism: to a belief that man is wise, good, and powerful enough to govern, perfect, and save himself. Humanism denies the infallibility of the Bible and man's need of God. This often incorporates beliefs such as atheism, evolution, situation ethics, and deification of humankind. Once we dismiss the Bible as the guide for our lives, we become susceptible to unconscionable acts, not only from distorted thinking but also from Satan himself. Nothing is sacred, and nothing is sinful. That is how tyrants such as Adolf Hitler and Saddam Hussein and madmen such as Osama bin Laden and Charles Manson justify their deeds. So we digress to gas chambers for adult overpopulation and abortion clinics for unwanted infants and mass slayings for the infidels and Helter Skelter murders to produce race wars. Further, humanistic philosophy prepares the way for a worldwide government and the reign of a one-world leader: the Antichrist will accommodate this secular philosophy.

Saving faith is more than an acknowledging faith; it is an obedient faith, or faith in action. By faith Abel offered a sacrifice, by faith Enoch pleased God, by faith Noah prepared an ark, by faith Abraham obeyed the command of God (Hebrews 11:4-8). True saving faith causes us to obey God's Word, bringing salvation through the blood of Jesus Christ. Prior to Calvary, saving faith constituted abiding by God-ordained mandates: a moral conscience, obedience to the voice of God (God spoke directly to selected individuals: Noah, Abraham, Moses), obedience to the Law of Moses, and adherence to the directives of the prophets regarding repentance and righteousness. After Calvary, saving faith constituted obeying the message of Christ and His apostles as recorded in the New Testament. From Scripture we readily see how throughout the ages mankind is saved through obedient faith.

In his letter to the Ephesian church, Paul proclaimed, "For by grace are ye saved through faith; and that not of yourselves: it is the gift of God: not of works, lest any man should boast" (Ephesians 2:8-9). Does this passage suggest we are saved merely by an acknowledging faith? To the contrary, a study of grace and faith reveals both to be active verbs. Grace expresses man's inability to restore himself to his original state in the Garden of Eden. God does for man what he can't do for himself: grace. Only God's grace can change man's fallen state and restore him to the presence of God. However, this isn't a blanket arrangement all experience because Christ went to Calvary. Grace is extended to all, but it only affects those who act upon its provisions: saving grace. Mankind is saved through an obedient faith in God and His Word.

How did God in His omniscience, knowing mankind would sin, justify following through with the creation? Why didn't He stop with the animal kingdom? Let's consider an analogy to better understand this perplexity. An architect designing an apartment complex must contend with the possibility that many lives could be lost if the building caught on fire. At this point he can do one of three things: scrap the blueprints altogether, proceed with the drawings and assume no personal responsibility for the occupants, or design safety features, especially a fire escape, into the project. In creation, the Lord chose the third alternative; He planned a way of escape for fallen man. However, man must act upon God's plan. This is the meaning of the phrase "saved by grace." Salvation is God's gift to us. Man did not and could not initiate a plan of salvation. God Himself chose to come in flesh and as a man to suffer, bleed, and die for the sins of the world. We did not merit salvation: "For all have sinned, and come short of the glory of God" (Romans 3:23). God incorporated grace into His creative plan. Further, grace as the gift of God doesn't suggest we have no responsibility to resist sin in our lives. We do not diminish grace when we show our appreciation for salvation by serving the Lord with our whole being. In fact, Scripture teaches us to do so. Paul exhorted the Romans, "Be ye transformed..." (Romans 12:2). The Greek word for transformed is the same word used to express the transfiguration of Christ (Matthew 17:2). The word literally means to allow what is within a person to become visible outwardly. The transfiguration of Christ allowed Peter, James, and John to perceive the deity of Christ in addition to His humanity. Since the Roman Christians had partaken of the grace of God and possessed within their hearts the heavenly gift of God, they were to manifest it outwardly in daily living.

No one can earn salvation; it's the gift of God, but even a gift must be accepted, activated, or unwrapped. This is accomplished by our obedient faith. Each example of salvation expressed in Scripture is accompanied by some act of obedient faith. With each example of someone receiving God's grace, there is also the expectation that person will manifest a life of good works. To the adulterous woman Christ directed, "...Neither do I condemn thee: go, and sin no more" (John 8:11). The changed lifestyle expresses appreciation for God's grace and becomes a witness of God's transforming power in the life of the believer. The Bible enjoins us to manifest good works: "Let your light so shine before men, that they may see your good works, and glorify your Father which is in heaven" (Matthew 5:16). "Be rich in good works" (1 Timothy 6:18). "In all things shewing thyself a pattern of good works" (Titus 2:7). "Faith, if it hath not works, is dead, being alone... shew me thy faith without thy works, and I will shew thee my faith by my works" (James 2:17). "Therefore to him that knoweth to do good, and doeth it not, to him it is sin" (James 4:17).

After sin broke man's fellowship with God, man could not restore that fellowship by any amount of good works: sin tainted man in a way he had no personal means of recovering. Enter God! God purchased salvation for man and by His grace restores believers to fellowship with Him. Once this reconciliation occurs, God expects man to pursue an overcoming life. "Walk worthy of the vocation wherewith ye are called (Ephesians 4:1). "Walk worthy of the Lord... being fruitful in every good work" (Colossians 1:10). "Walk after his commandments" (II John 6). The Bible clearly teaches the believer to overcome sin. Not only does it tell us to overcome, it tells us how to overcome.

God gladly forgives confessed sins, but He takes no pleasure in continual confession of sins we have not conquered. Paul challenged the Roman Christians by asking, "Shall we continue in sin, that grace may abound?" (Romans (6:1). He immediately answered his own question with two words, "God forbid" (Romans 6:2). He further explained his reasoning:

> Knowing this, that our old man is crucified with him, that the body of sin might be destroyed, that henceforth we should not serve sin. For he that is dead is freed from sin. Now if we be dead with Christ, we believe that we shall also live with him: Knowing that Christ being raised from the dead

dieth no more; death hath no more dominion over him. For in that he died, he died unto sin once: but in that he liveth, he liveth unto God. Likewise reckon ye also yourselves to be dead indeed unto sin, but alive unto God through Jesus Christ our Lord. Let not sin therefore reign in your mortal body, that ye should obey it in the lusts thereof.

Romans 6:6-12

God's redemptive plan has a twofold benefit. Not only did God establish a plan to forgive man's past sins, but He also instituted a plan to give man victory over future temptations to sin. God made provision, through the instruction of His Word and the power of the indwelling Spirit, for the Christian to live a continual life of victory over sin.

Points of Discussion

Discuss the consequences of the Fall in the Garden of Eden.

Why can mankind not save himself?

Discuss the difference between "acknowledging" faith and "saving" faith.

How does Christ's death pay our debt of sin?

CHAPTER 5

Why The Struggle?

Since God knows we love Him, why does He send temptations? Why does a loving God permit temptations from a wicked spirit being? Many sincere Christians have struggled with these questions. To answer them we first need to establish a very important biblical concept: The Lord does not tempt us to sin. Period.

God desires to give good gifts to His children, not temptations to sin. "Let no man say when he is tempted, I am tempted of God: for God cannot be tempted with evil, neither tempteth he any man. But every man is tempted, when he is drawn away of his own lust, and enticed" (James 1:13-14). If God should choose, He could cause every one of us to break under His pressure. We would all miserably fail Him. God doesn't desire to make life difficult for us; neither is it pleasurable for Him to see us struggle with life's perplexities, nor does He follow us around like a policeman trailing a suspected criminal. God is not seeking to eliminate us from heaven's roll book; conversely, He delights in our salvation and wants us to go to heaven.

God loves the whole world, sinners as well as saints, Communists as well as proponents of democracy. God desires for all to be saved. His plan for reaching the world is for the church to take the message of salvation to all mankind. He leaves His church in the world for a while that we might win the world to Him for eternity.

Our struggles arise from several sources. First, we receive temptations to sin from Satan, this evil world, and the flesh (sinful nature) within us. The resulting battle is not part of an endless struggle between two evenly matched superpowers—God and Satan—with mankind caught helplessly in the middle. To the contrary Satan is already defeated, and God will soon end the conflict by restraining Satan forever. Satan's timeline is set, and his future is sealed; yet he acts as though he can win the war. He has dispatched his army of seasoned warriors even to the smallest hamlets, as if he could conquer the earth and destroy God's influence here. Consequently, both saint and sinner daily confront the allurements of sin, which appeal to the flesh. Even the child of God, who has Christ's nature, also has a sinful nature that Satan's temptations can attract.

How can one have both the nature of Christ and a sinful nature? The sinful nature is the fallen nature of Adam still resident within all mankind. How then do we reconcile Paul's explanation regarding the old man? "Therefore if any man be in Christ, he is a new creature: old things are passed away; behold, all things are become new" (2 Corinthians 5:17). The Christian's new birth does not give him new flesh but new priorities. The new birth does not eliminate the old, sinful nature, but it does impart a new nature, which can override the old nature and control the Christian's decisions. This new nature is the nature of Christ, or the indwelling Spirit. Thus a struggle between good and evil takes place within the Christian's life (See Galatians 5:16-25). This struggle continues until death or until Christ translates us from earth to glory.

Second, some struggles stem from the trials and hardships of life, which we must endure to grow spiritually. An elderly friend once related a personal experience that illustrates this concept. In his back yard was an apple tree that did not produce. Every spring the tree blossomed in abundance, but at harvest time there were no apples to pluck. My friend met a self-taught botanist, an aged Indian who had spent a lifetime experimenting with various plants and trees, and he called upon his assistance. After examining the unfruitful tree he proclaimed, "You've been feeding this tree too much." The owner admitted that he'd continually fertilized the apple tree in hopes of enriching its fruit yield. The Indian explained that as long as the apple tree's life was not in danger, there was no inbred call for reproduction. He suggested my friend drive nails into the roots of the tree. Reluctantly he complied. The next year there was a tremendous apple yield.

Likewise, a threat to one's life brings out the survival instinct. The same is true in a spiritual sense. Trials force us into a deeper relationship with God: Bible reading, devotion, and prayer. We reach out to Him for answers and for strength. The closer we draw to Him, the more like Him we become. We no longer pray, "When will I get out of this trial?" but "What will I get out of this trial?" Soon we see the world through God's eyes—lost and headed for eternal judgment. We begin to reproduce spiritual children, thus fulfilling God's purpose for allowing us to remain in this world.

In the original Greek New Testament there are two words for temptation: *dokimaze* and *peirazo*. These are translated into the English words test, try, tempt, and prove, but the original Greek words have deeper meaning than is understood by these words. *Dokimaze* refers to the testing of one's life to show one's qualities. According to Wuest, "The word refers to the act of testing someone or something for the purpose of approving it."[8] The Bible uses this word to describe the Lord's testing of us. The purpose of this testing is not to tempt us to sin but to bring out the good within us. God examines us in order to elevate us. This type of examination will take place at the judgment seat of Christ (1 Corinthians 3:13-15; Romans 14:10). This testing is not for the sake of condemnation but for elevation. This test approves the church as the bride of Christ. The same Greek word is used regarding testing that precedes the rapture. It refers to experiences while in this life. For reasons sometimes known only to Him, such tests are God's approval upon our lives; they are His vote of confidence in us. For this type of test we should give thanks. The Lord's testing confirms we are growing as a Christian. Like a proud parent displaying the abilities of a maturing child, God takes pleasure in our spiritual progress and worth to His Kingdom.

Dokimaze isn't used to describe satanic temptations. In contrast, the Bible uses the Greek word *peirozo* to describe the temptations from Satan. This word is used in a sense of "finding one's weakness for the sake of destruction." Of course, the devil wants us to break under the pressure he applies to our weaknesses. Still, the Bible also uses *peirazo* for the Lord's dealings with the believer. When used in this way it doesn't suggest to "find one's weakness for the sake of destroying;" contrariwise, it is to help the believer discover a weakness so he will trust in the Lord for power to overcome the weakness. I heard a wise minister explain, "The Lord knows what you are. He wants you to know what you are."[9] We should thank God for tests He allows, for they motivate us to become more like Christ. James, the brother of Christ, expressed three principles regarding temptation: accept temptation with gratitude; temptations work toward our good; God does not send temptation to harm us.

> My brethren, count it all joy when ye fall into divers temptations; Knowing this, that the trying of your faith worketh patience. Blessed is the man that endureth temptation: for when he is tried, he shall receive the crown of life, which the Lord hath promised to them that love him. Let no man say when he is tempted, I am tempted of God: for God cannot be tempted with evil, neither tempteth he any man: But every man is tempted, when he is drawn away of his own lust, and enticed.
>
> James 1:2-3, 12-14

The Greek terms for temptation explain that temptations sent or allowed by the Lord are never for our destruction but for our spiritual growth. God sends and allows trials in order to reveal our weaknesses so we can work on them or for some positive good of which we may be unaware. Each time we recognize and correct problems in our lives, we become better and more profitable soldiers in the Lord's army. Ultimately, we will receive an eternal reward.

We can better understand temptation if we're aware of the uniqueness of the original terms used. The Septuagint translators used the word *peirozo* in the account of Abraham's testing. "And it came to pass after these things, that God did tempt Abraham." (Genesis 22:1). God did not tempt Abraham to sin but tested him for the sake of the purpose of his calling. The words "after these things" help explain the reason for the test. In Genesis 12, God had commanded Abraham to do four things: (1) leave his country, (2) leave his kindred, (3) leave his father's house, and (4) go to a land that God would show him. With the four commands, God promised to do four things for Abraham: (1) make him a great nation, (2) bless him (with material blessings), (3) make his name great, and (4) make him a blessing to all the earth (by the promised Messiah coming through his lineage). To receive God's promises, man must meet God's conditions. According to Genesis 11:31-32, Abraham hadn't fully complied with God's commands, and thus he was not yet entitled to receive God's promises.

It seems God demanded more than a geographical relocation: it included associations. If this was true, consider Abraham's shortcomings. He didn't leave his father, Terah, who was an idolater (Joshua 24:2). Nor did Abraham leave his kindred. Instead, his nephew Lot accompanied him. Moreover, God intended for Abraham to relocate in Canaan, but Abraham stopped in Haran. This was approximately six hundred miles from his home in Ur but still four hundred miles short of his destination. God didn't settle for these compromises. For Abraham to be the father of the faithful, he first had to be faithful.

With Abraham, as sometimes with us, compliance regarding God's instructions came over time. His father eventually died, and Abraham finally moved to Canaan. Once in Canaan, it was probably years before he separated from his nephew Lot. These events seemingly came by coincidence or divine intervention but not because of Abraham's faithfulness. To prove His faithfulness, God gave Abraham a son before Abraham completely obeyed the covenant commands. God knew Abraham's unrealized potential and continued to work in Abraham's life, even though he settled into a comfortable insignificance. For Abraham to receive the full reward of the faithful, however, he had to exhibit an unwavering faith.

God patiently guides us to a point of faith. Until this time, for Abraham, that mountain peak loomed in the horizon, allusive and unattainable. The God of a second chance (and third and fourth and fifth) gave Abraham another opportunity when He commanded, "Take now thy son, thine only son Isaac, whom thou lovest, and get thee into the land of Moriah; and offer him there for a burnt offering upon one of the mountains which I will tell thee of" (Genesis 22:2). Failed tests never get easier, but they always include a singular principle: God's love. God never intended to hurt either Abraham or Isaac. In contrast, He wanted to fulfill His promises to Abraham, but up to this point Abraham had not passed the examination: he wasn't ready for God's promotion.

Trials are not vicious acts of a sadistic God. They are God's means of preparing our lives for some significant purpose. For Abraham, this ultimate trial was an opportunity for him to receive the blessings God longed to give. It was an opportunity for Abraham to examine his flawed character, to perceive his faulty decision making, to shed his fears, and to fully trust God's every promise. There's a lot about God's demand upon Abraham we don't fully understand. Human sacrifice was never asked of anyone before or since and is denounced by Scripture, but Abraham passed the test. The best we can explain the strange demand of God upon Abraham is to realize the similarities of Abraham's story to the story of Calvary. Immediately God announced Abraham's score and affirmed him worthy to receive the original promises. The demand of human sacrifice was revoked. A substitute animal sacrifice miraculously appeared. An angel proclaimed:

> Because thou hast done this thing, and hast not withheld thy son, thine only son: that in blessing I will bless thee, and in multiplying I will multiply thy seed as the stars of the heaven, and as the sand which is upon the sea shore; and thy seed shall possess the gate of his enemies; and in thy seed shall all the nations of the earth be blessed; because thou hast obeyed my voice.
>
> Genesis 22:16-18

Some misunderstand the love of God and question how a loving God would send trials upon His children. They view God's love and His trials as incompatible. The writer of the New Testament Book of Hebrews explains, however, that permissiveness is not love. Rather, permissiveness usually indicates a shirking of responsibility.

And ye have forgotten the exhortation which speaketh unto you as unto children, My son, despise not thou the chastening of the Lord, nor faint when thou art rebuked of him: For whom the Lord loveth he chasteneth, and scourgeth every son whom he receiveth. If ye endure chastening, God dealeth with you as with sons; for what son is he whom the father chasteneth not? But if ye be without chastisement, whereof all are partakers, then are ye bastards, and not sons. Furthermore we have had fathers of our flesh which corrected us, and we gave them reverence: shall we not much rather be in subjection unto the Father of spirits, and live? For they verily for a few days chastened us after their own pleasure; but he for our profit, that we might be partakers of his holiness. Now no chastening for the present seemeth to be joyous, but grievous: nevertheless afterward it yieldeth the peaceable fruit of righteousness unto them which are exercised thereby.

Hebrews 12:5-11

Research projects suggest that the best parents are those who express a great deal of love to their children but who also maintain firm discipline. Likewise, because God loves us, He has established guidelines for our lives. These are for our good. At times, these disciplines may seem burdensome, but the omniscient God is planning for our eternal welfare, not the immediate gratification of our earthly desires.

For a child to become a disciplined, responsible adult, his parents must teach him while he is still a child to pick up his toys and to wash behind his ears. No explanation is necessary from the parent. This teaching may not seem joyous or important to the child at the time, but the loving, caring parent is looking after the child's future. Likewise, God trains us for the future by putting us through present situations that may seem burdensome and frightful. No explanation is necessary from the Lord. He does this for our development—not for our hurt—because He loves us.

Will Durant wrote regarding the Roman Empire, that it "...remained great as long as she had enemies who forced her to unity, vision, and heroism. When she had overcome them all she flourished for a moment and then began to die."[10] We need obstacles. These serve as stepping stones and not stumbling blocks. Trials from the Lord are merely growing pains, not debilitating charley horses. Difficulties are essential for maturation in Christian service.

When Israel received freedom from Egyptian bondage, they assumed that within a few weeks they would enter the Promised Land. Instead of a direct northeast route, God sent them southeast into the wilderness of Sinai. Why? They weren't ready to enter the Promised Land. They lacked a love for and a faith in the very God who delivered them from bondage. The ten miracles of deliverance didn't change their calloused hearts of unbelief. God had to change their four hundred years of Egypt-molding carnality into a God-believing spirituality. They possessed too much of Egypt and too little of *Elohim*. They weren't ready to trust *Yahweh*: the "I Am That I Am" who sent Moses to deliver them. God had to transform them into a people who could enter Canaan. It took only a few days for Israel to leave Egypt, but it took forty years to get Egypt out of their hearts. This came about through the wilderness tests. Israel's wilderness wanderings parallel the Christian's current struggles. God is getting us ready for the future "giants" we need to conquer. There are lessons we need to learn that we can only learn through struggle.

The first lesson Israel had to learn, and we must learn the same lesson, is that God is in complete control of our lives. Shortly after their departure from Egypt, the Israelites found themselves trapped by the impassible Red Sea and the rapidly approaching Egyptian Army. In this seemingly hopeless situation, the Israelites watched helplessly as God brought miraculous victory out of their first trial. God granted them deliverance through the same Red Sea that drowned the pursuing enemy.

After this miraculous escape from the Egyptian army, the Israelites still needed to learn continual dependence on God. They soon realized that if they continued long in the barren Sinai Peninsula, they needed an abundant supply of food and water. Someone calculated that supplying food and water for three to five million Israelites would have taken one hundred and sixty box cars of food and over a thousand tank cars of water every day.[11] God miraculously supplied them with food and water—not just for a day, or even for forty days—for forty years.

In the wilderness Israel also learned the need to depend on one another. During the battle with Amalek, Aaron and Hur joined together to hold up the tired arms of Moses. From a high mountain perch they viewed the battle raging below. As they held the arms of Moses aloft, Joshua and the army of Israel defeated their enemy. The battle required more than individual effort. Victory came only through unity. Many today haven't learned this lesson well enough, and some not at all. Too many Christian believers operate not unlike the cancer cell, which cares only for itself, not realizing its dependence on other cells. It "continues its reckless and egocentric development, feeding on its host until it kills it—and so commits suicide."[12]

When problems come our way, however, we begin to learn the true value of a praying parent or a caring friend. While some Israelites were destroyed in the wilderness because of their rebellion, others were able to recognize their need of spiritual leadership. Often, struggles are necessary to bring us to a place of humility and subjection to those who "watch for your souls" (Hebrews 13:17). We recognize the value of a pastor or a friend who isn't afraid to challenge our flawed thought process.

Further, in the trial of bitter waters at Marah, Israel learned, "… I am the LORD that healeth thee" (Exodus 15:26). Likewise, sickness can draw us nearer to Christ, as we depend upon His stripes for our healing. We cannot experience the power of God's healing until we first suffer the pain of sickness.

Many times we fail to accept what God is trying to teach us, so we must go back to the wilderness for more schooling. This was the case with Israel. God intended for a few weeks of wilderness trials to teach total reliance upon His love, mercy, and provision. The few weeks turned into forty years. They were slow learners: some never learned to trust and obey God and thus died in the wilderness, a few miles short of the promise land.

Finally, some tests simply come as a consequence of the circumstances surrounding us. Because we live on planet Earth, all of us—saint and sinner alike—experience certain difficulties which have no predetermined purpose of the Lord and may be an attack from the adversary, our sworn enemy, Satan. The Apostle Peter admonished us to resist the devil, whose goal is to destroy us, "… knowing that the same afflictions are accomplished in your brethren that are in the world [unbelievers]" (I Peter 5:8-9). The adversary of the soul confronts all mankind, but the believer is at an advantage. We can address Satan's temptations in a manner that can be beneficial in our Christian life. The Apostle Peter further states, "But the God of all grace, who hath called us unto his eternal glory by Christ Jesus, after that ye have suffered a while, make you perfect, stablish, strengthen, settle you" (I Peter 5:10). Temptations that drive the unbeliever farther into despair and sin, and eventually overcome him, can benefit the believer. The Christian can turn temptation to his advantage and become stronger in the Lord by learning to rely upon God's grace and strength for deliverance.

In summary, Christians need to understand six truths concerning temptation:

1. God does not tempt us to cause us to sin. "Let no man say when he is tempted, I am tempted of God: for God cannot be tempted with evil, neither tempteth he any man" (James 1:13). God wants us to be saved, and He wants to bless us.

2. In every temptation, there will always be a way of escape. "There hath no temptation taken you but such as is common to man: but God is faithful, who will not suffer you to be tempted above that ye are able; but will with the temptation also make a way to escape, that ye may be able to bear it" (I Corinthians 10:13). Either we will be able to overcome the temptation or else God will prevent it from coming to us. God will not allow Satan to tempt us beyond our ability to overcome. Should we fail, the Lord forgives if we seek forgiveness. "If we confess our sins, he is faithful and just to forgive us our sins, and to cleanse us from all unrighteousness" (I John 1:9).

3. Blessings always follow trials. God will turn the seeming hardship into something beneficial for us. "And we know that all things work together for good to them that love God, to them who are the called according to his purpose" (Romans 8:28). The Lord

allowed Satan to tempt Job, but Job received twice the mount of blessings after his trial as he had before.

4. God sends trials to teach us to rely upon His power and to strengthen us in our Christian walk. The struggle required to overcome temptation is good for us as it develops spiritual stamina. Adversity is a necessary part of the normal process of development. Diamonds and graphite are composed of the same substance: carbon. The only difference in the two is their molecular structure, which is determined by the amount of pressure applied to each. Diamonds have been exposed to a tremendous amount of pressure, but graphite has not. God may want us to be diamonds in His Kingdom; if so, in order for this to happen, a certain element of pressure must be applied.

5. Simply because we live in this world, trials and tribulations will inevitably come, whether we are Christians or not. We can either surrender to the devil and lose our souls, or we can trust the Lord for victory (I Peter 5:5-10). Unquestionably, we should choose the latter alternative.

6. Temptation itself is not sin. Jesus was tempted in all points as we are, yet without sin (Hebrews 4:15). Evil thoughts and sinful desires may knock at our heart's door, but this is not sin in itself. These are temptations; these are normal life experiences. We don't sin unless we yield to these temptations, whether by entertaining and enjoying them in the mind or by enacting them physically.

Where do we start? A great starting point is to pray as the Lord taught, "… And lead us not into temptation; but deliver us from evil." (Luke 11:4). Overcoming is not always easy, but it is always possible. We can be overcomers.

Points of Discussion

Discuss the different areas from which temptations come.

James 1:13 states the Lord does not tempt us, yet Genesis 22:1 states that God tempted Abraham. Discuss the difference between the two statements.

Why does God permit, and even send, trials into our lives?

Discuss the assurances of our victory over temptation.

CHAPTER 6

Initial Encounter

M ost can vividly recall the first encounter with temptation after being born again. For many it comes as a great surprise, but it should not. You are not to blame, and there is no way to prevent all temptation. Trials are certain to come. The Apostle Peter warned us, "Beloved, think it not strange concerning the fiery trial which is to try you, as though some strange thing happened unto you" (I Peter 4:12). This Scripture helps to counteract the emotional pressure that arises from the first encounter with temptation. Moreover, when we succumb to temptation and commit sin, we are driven into a sense of despair. I find it interesting that the emotions related to spiritual failure somewhat parallel those related to the Kübler-Ross Model of facing natural death.[13] The following emotional reactions often follow the first temptation, especially when we yield to the temptation:

SHOCK. How can a Christian be tempted? "I thought the new birth eradicated the sinful nature. I thought I was dead to sin and, therefore, free from temptation. How can I be a Christian and be tempted by sin? I must not have gotten enough of God. I may not have even gotten saved in the first place."

55

GUILT. After the initial feeling of shock has subsided, guilt slithers in. "I've displeased God and brought shame to Him. I must not have guarded my life properly. I must be a weaker Christian than most, or maybe I'm just a hypocrite! Certainly other Christians don't experience such temptations, and definitely they don't yield to the temptation."

DOUBT. At this point Satan really begins to work on the mind. "Perhaps I didn't experience genuine salvation. Could it have been my own emotions rather than the Holy Spirit baptism? Maybe the entire salvation experience was just pretense on my part. Perhaps the Bible is not true, and the salvation message came from man's imagination or deception."

ANGER. Different forms of anger will often surface. The new Christian may point an accusing finger at another. "If others had been more sensitive to my needs, perhaps I wouldn't have failed." Emotional outbursts often prevail over rational reactions. Frustration mounts into an "A-Bomb" (Anger Bomb) explosion, with verbalizations one really doesn't mean.

DEPRESSION. Waves of depression ultimately follow. The Christian focuses all the anger and disappointment upon himself. "I must be a poor Christian to allow such thoughts and actions." Or, "I have actually stooped to the point of sinning against the Lord. I might as well give up! I have shamed Christ, and I can never change that." And finally, the ultimate thought of defeat, "I'll never be able overcome my sin."

We must combat these reactions vigorously, and at the least, arrive at the final stage of the Kübler-Ross Model of facing death: acceptance. This is not a stage of resigning to fate. It is acceptance of reality.

ACCEPTANCE. The reality of a Christian failing God is to accept not only the fact that we have failed but also that there is provision for our sins. The provision is Calvary. We revisit Calvary through repentance. At Calvary we always find forgiveness. Period. No exceptions. It's the promise of Scripture (I John 1:9).

God never promised us freedom from temptation in this life. In fact, His Word warns us of the certainty of temptation. We are in the battle whether we like it or not. Remember the apostle's warning, "Beloved, think it not strange concerning the fiery trial which is to try you, as though some strange thing happened unto you" (I Peter 4:12). Further, the Scripture warns of the ever-abiding old nature that wars against the new nature of Christ we acquire at the New Birth: "If we say that we have no sin, we deceive ourselves, and the truth is not in us. If we say that we have not sinned, we make him a liar, and his word is not in us" (I John 1:8, 10). Christ made provision for us if we fail the temptation. We'll discuss that in depth later in the book.

When a trial comes, we should not see it as a defeat; rather, we should view it as the norm. First, it affirms God's Word. We are a fallen humanity needing a Savior. Next, trials are an affirmation of our identity with Christ, which makes us a target of Satan. The time has arrived for us to participate in Christ's sufferings, to be involved on His team, to take a stand against the flesh. Our association with Christ is a guarantee of temptation. "But rejoice, inasmuch as ye are partakers of Christ's sufferings; that, when his glory shall be revealed, ye may be glad also with exceeding joy" (I Peter 4:13). Both the saint and the sinner are subject to temptation, but the born-again believer doesn't face trials alone. Christ joins us to confront our temptation. Before, we met temptation alone and failed. Christ met temptation alone but overcame (Hebrews 4:15). Now, we face temptation again; only this time we face it together with Christ. This time we can overcome as Christ overcame. We don't overcome through our own power but through the power of the resurrected Savior, Jesus Christ.

The confusion and personal disappointment that often follows initial temptation, especially if one fails the test, come because of a false concept of the New Birth experience. New Christians sometimes confuse spiritual rebirth with the glorification that will take place at the Second Coming of Christ. The New Birth does not change the flesh! Our flesh remains flesh. We still get burned if we touch a hot stove, and a hammer blow to the finger still causes pain. Likewise, the sinful nature has not been eradicated; rather, the New Birth brings the potential to subdue the will of the old nature. We are still susceptible to the temptations that plagued us before we received the Holy Spirit. The old nature is still present within us, but for the first time we have the nature of Christ which combats the old nature. For the born-again believer, the flesh (sinful nature) and Spirit (new nature) are at war in our lives. Our responsibility is not to seek elimination of the old nature; rather, it is to subdue the flesh through the power of the Holy Spirit. The Apostle Paul instructed:

> This I say then, Walk in the Spirit, and ye shall not fulfil the lust of the flesh. For the flesh lusteth against the Spirit, and the Spirit against the flesh: and these are contrary the one to the other: so that ye cannot do the things that ye would. But if ye be led of the Spirit, ye are not under the law. Now the works of the flesh are manifest, which are these; adultery, fornication, uncleanness, lasciviousness, idolatry, witchcraft, hatred, variance, emulations, wrath, strife, seditions, heresies, envyings, murders, drunkenness, revellings, and such like: of the which I tell you before, as I have also told you in time past, that they which do such things shall not inherit the kingdom of God. But the fruit of the Spirit is love, joy, peace, longsuffering, gentleness, goodness, faith, meekness, temperance: against such there is no law. And they that are Christ's have crucified the flesh with the affections and lusts. If we live in the Spirit, let us also walk in the Spirit.

Galatians 5:16-25

We still must choose between pursuing good and pursuing evil. Once we make a choice to follow the things of God, we have the resident Spirit of Christ to subdue the fleshly desires and grow the spiritual desires.

We dare not be overwhelmed by a failure to overcome—disappointed but not overwhelmed. Nor must we succumb to the aftermath of Satan's condemnation. Such unearned guilt is best dealt with by confession and accepting Christ's loving sacrifice for our sins. We must realize we are engaged in a war, not of our personal doing, and wars aren't lost by a single battle but by a series of defeats followed by surrender. We are defeated only if we surrender to the flesh and walk away from the indwelling Spirit of Christ. Neither should we weary of the length of the battle. The war between the flesh and the Spirit will continue as long as we are in the world, but there is an end to the conflict. Our fleshly nature will be changed when Christ calls us home, but not until then. At that time, mortality will put on immortality, and the fleshly nature will be eradicated forever.

> Behold, I shew you a mystery; we shall not all sleep, but we shall all be changed, in a moment, in the twinkling of an eye, at the last trump: for the trumpet shall sound, and the dead shall be raised incorruptible, and we shall be changed. For this corruptible must put on incorruption, and this mortal must put on immortality. So when this corruptible shall have put on incorruption, and this mortal shall have put on immortality, then shall be brought to pass the saying that is written, "Death is swallowed up in victory."

> I Corinthians 15:51-54

This change will make it impossible to ever be tempted and to ever sin in heaven—one of the reasons why heaven will be so heavenly. We are awaiting that glorious transformation, but until the resurrection takes place, we must contend with temptations.

When we were born again, we received the indwelling Spirit of Christ, which makes it possible to overcome satanic and fleshly temptations. We did not, however, receive immunity from temptation, but for the first time we received power to resist temptation and to conquer sin. Jesus said, "In the world ye shall have tribulation: but he of good cheer; I have overcome the world" (John 16:33). As He was tempted, we are tempted; likewise, as He overcame, we overcome through His abiding presence. He paved the way, shows the way, and guides us along the way.

By way of Incarnation, Jesus Christ possessed a dual nature. He was both God and man. His humanity did not limit His deity, but His humanity possessed the same qualities as ours, except for sin. He had a complete human nature like that of Adam in the state of innocence, but He didn't possess the fallen, sinful nature of Adam. Christ's body was not conceived of sinful man; conversely, the Holy Spirit miraculously conceived Christ. Christ was without sin. Nevertheless, He experienced the same temptations we do in that He had a will to choose. In this respect He was like Adam before the fall.

The difference between Christ and us: we have an inner craving for the things that are sinful. We operate from a self-centered character. The flawless attributes which Adam received from God died when he partook of sin. In contrast, the vacuum created by this spiritual death was filled with the traits of mankind's new master: hate, bitterness, jealousy, envy.

Adam's creation from a scoop of dust in God's hand and Christ's conception of the Holy Spirit had two commonalities. First, both Adam and Christ had a human nature that included the right to choose to follow after righteousness. Neither was robotic in nature. Second, they were sinless. The first Adam was created perfect, without a sinful nature; likewise, the second Adam, Christ, had a pure nature, untainted because of Divine conception.

The New Testament writer describes Christ's humanity when he expressed, "For we have not an high priest which cannot be touched with the feeling of our infirmities; but was in all points tempted like as we are, yet without sin" (Hebrews 4:15). Unlike our temptations, the temptations of Christ didn't come from inner desire for sin; rather, like the temptation of Adam, who had no knowledge of sin, Satan introduced temptations that were pleasurable in nature. In both cases the external temptations appealed to the flesh. "And when the woman saw that the tree was good for food, and that it was pleasant to the eyes, and a tree to be desired to make one wise, she took of the fruit thereof, and did eat, and gave also unto her husband with her; and he did eat" (Genesis 3:6). When Satan tempted Christ, he offered bread to satisfy His hunger, a dare to challenge His Deity, and a kingdom to reflect His throne. Unlike Adam, Christ never yielded to these temptations.

In addition to reconciling man back to God, Jesus Christ's sinless life demonstrated two principles regarding the creation. First, Adam and Eve didn't have to yield to the serpent's lies. In their perfect state they could have resisted Satan's temptation. Though mislead by Satan's subtlety, they could have conferred with the Lord, who visited with them seemingly on a daily basis. God would have gladly exposed to them Satan's ploy. Further, if they had requested intervention, God would have expelled Satan from the garden. The second principle Christ proved is that born-again believers, because of the indwelling Christ, do not have to yield to temptations. Remember the promise of Scripture (I Corinthians 10:13; I John 4:4). We can be overcomers.

The Apostle Peter warned that Christianity does not exempt us from trials.

> Humble yourselves therefore under the mighty hand of God, that he may exalt you in due time: casting all your care upon him; for he careth for you. Be sober, be vigilant; because your adversary the devil, as a roaring lion, walketh about, seeking whom he may devour: whom resist stedfast in the faith, knowing that the same afflictions are accomplished in your brethren that are in the world. But the God of all grace, who hath called us unto his eternal glory by Christ Jesus, after that ye have suffered a while, make you perfect, stablish, strengthen, settle you.
>
> 1 Peter 5:6-10

In the above passage of Scripture we can discern three rules to follow in times of temptation. The Three R's of Temptation: Recognize! Rely! Resist!

Recognition

We must recognize what is happening. The struggle exists for two reasons. First, Satan does not want anyone to be saved. When someone is born again, Satan has lost another soul to Calvary. He is unwilling to concede defeat, and he wants that person back. Second, we are still flesh. Our body is not yet glorified; we are still susceptible to temptation. The struggle between Spirit and flesh will continue until Jesus takes us out of this world.

We must not allow ourselves to be caught in a guilt trip when temptation comes; instead, we should thank God that He has enough confidence in us, as He did in Job, to allow Satan to tempt us. We can use temptation to remind us of the forgiveness of past sins and to remind us of the promise of victory over present and future temptations. We should thank God for His overcoming power within us and for His molding, polishing, and perfecting work in our lives.

Reliance

Next, we must rely upon the Lord. We must pray, being honest with ourselves regarding our vulnerability, and we should admit to Him our weaknesses. We must express our dependence upon the Holy Spirit for power to overcome. Adam and Eve could have overcome temptation by relying on God's help. God was literally with them in the Garden of Eden. Just because they did not see Him did not mean He was absent, and His frequent visitations should have reinforced His continued concern for them. They could have called upon Him for counsel, and Satan would have fled. We must not make the same mistake they made, thinking we are alone or that God isn't being totally truthful regarding life. Instead, we should call upon God.

Christ walked the path of life before us, and He walks it with us at the very moment of temptation. Not only does Christ sympathize with us, but He is also our source of strength. He not only hears our prayers, but He also answers them. While on earth, Christ prayed that God would keep us from the evil of the world, "I pray not that thou shouldest take them out of the world, but that thou shouldest keep them from the evil. Neither pray I for these alone, but for them also which shall believe on me through their word" (John 17:15, 20). Christ now reigns supreme, responsible in His deity for answering the prayer He prayed in His humanity.

We can rely upon the promises of God. We should know and believe these promises. The Word of God, which is forever settled in heaven and cannot be altered, assures us of our ability to defeat temptation. We should memorize and apply in our Christian walk I Corinthians 10:13. Our temptation is common to man; others have experienced it and have overcome, and so can we. Also, God is faithful, and He refuses to let us be tempted beyond our ability to withstand the temptation. With every attack of the devil, there is an escape route. The escape route may include changing our social groups, places of entertainment, or reading habits; nevertheless, there will always be a way of escape from temptation.

Resistance

Finally, we must resist the devil, not of our personal authority, but in the name (authority) of the Lord. Michael the archangel, when contending with Satan, said simply, "The Lord rebuke thee" (Jude

9). When we call the name of the Lord in prayer, we invoke all the power of the One whose name we call. Jesus said, "If ye shall ask any thing in my name, I will do it" (John 14:14).

We also resist the devil by confession. First of all, we should confess to God our sins and need of divine intervention. If we are struggling with a particular problem, we can confess our faults to someone who can help us pray and can give us spiritual advice. The Scripture admonishes, "Confess your faults one to another, and pray one for another..." (James 5:16). It is possible to overcome without confession to another person; however, if we are struggling with overcoming a sin, we should never be too proud or too afraid to share our need of spiritual help with a mature, fellow believer.

As a word of caution, not every believer in which you may confide has wisdom and the ability to keep a confidence. For this reason and other reasons, some wait until they yield to temptation before they seek counsel, but it is always better to seek help first, before failing. We do not expect our children to bear a burden that is too heavy for them. We are God's children, and He feels the same way about us. Husband and wife should he able to share their struggles with one another. Young people need to be able to communicate with their parents. Everyone should rely on their pastor as a true friend, for he is willing and able to offer wisdom and strength.

The words of Sir Winston Churchill serve well as our ultimate response to temptation: "Never, never, never, never give up!"[14] God does not give up on us, so as long as we do not give up our position in Him, we have assurance of victory over sin. The battle is actually between Satan and the Lord, and we are on the Lord's side—because He wins, we win. He will not abandon us if we become wounded, but He will nurse us back to spiritual health so we can continue in His service. We may lose a battle, but that does not have to cost us the war. God has never been and can never be defeated. If we stay on His team, we may not be star players in our own eyes, but we will be winners nonetheless. There is no need to turn in our jerseys. The trophy will soon be given to the winning team, and we are on that team!

The nineteen-year-old young lady I mentioned in Chapter One gave up her struggle against temptation. She had a glorious Christian future ahead of her, but she gave up. If she had not, her natural singing ability would he enriching the worship of others today. Her son would still be attending church and learning of Christ and His love. Her husband may well have joined her in the Christian walk. In fact, a few weeks after his wife's surrender to temptation, he came for baptism. He came with regrets, certainly, but he came in sincerity, broken and ready to serve Christ.

Where did this sincere Christian lady go wrong? Why didn't she, like many others have, gain victory over her temptation? She did not follow the Lord's plan for overcoming temptation. She refused to walk through the doors provided for her escape. She rejected spiritual counsel, and, slowly but surely, her resistance against temptation weakened. She found herself seemingly unable to resist carnal desires. Such a tragic story does not need to be part of any Christian's life.

Many other Christians with similar problems as this young lady have sought out help that made the outcomes to their temptations victory stories. Through support of prayer, fellowship, and counseling, they overcame the adversary. They walk with the Lord today, demonstrating the overcoming power of Christ actively working in their lives. Our lives do not have to be stories of defeat but can be stories of victory. Each temptation brings us closer to the last. We can go from one victory to another until we receive ultimate victory at the rapture of the church. This isn't a fairy tale; it's the promise of Scripture and the will of our Savior.

Points of Discussion

Discuss the emotional reaction regarding temptation.

How can one who has truly experienced salvation still be tempted by sin?

Discuss how Christ, who was God, could be tempted by sin.

How may we apply the Three R's of Temptation?

CHAPTER 7

Preventive Maintenance

S ome years ago, I drove my car beyond its limits without having the front wheel bearings checked. Fifty miles from nowhere, the right front tire suddenly began to vibrate annoyingly. I drove on, stopping occasionally at my wife's urging and for fear of losing the wheel. Finally we could go no further. Six hours later, the total expense—including the towing bill—came to a hundred and sixty dollars. This was quite a price to pay for a neglected preventive measure costing fourteen dollars.

Few people practice preventive maintenance, but these few seldom find themselves stranded along the highway miles from home with an overheated engine and no water bucket. Some say it costs too much to service things before they break down. It does cost, but not too much. On the contrary, preventive maintenance saves in the long run.

Spiritual preventive maintenance can, likewise, spare us untold misery and defeat in time of temptation. This chapter discusses ways to maintain a strong spiritual life that prepares the Christian for the inevitable forthcoming temptations. The Biblical story of a young lady named Hannah, and her struggles to endure the trial of her faith, has great spiritual significance for us. Hannah, being childless for some time, longed for a child, but she remained barren. In Hannah's day, people considered childlessness somewhat like a curse. Each male greatly desired his lineage to continue, and Hannah's husband was no exception, so she longed for a baby boy to carry on the family name of her husband, Elkanah. The Bible says, however, "The Lord had shut up her womb" (I Samuel 1:5).

Added to Hannah's disappointment of barrenness was the rivalry of Elkanah's second wife, Peninnah. She delighted in reminding Hannah of her barrenness, for she had given birth to several children. In these trying circumstances, Hannah sought refuge in the house of God. In anguish of spirit she knelt and prayed. The priest Eli misinterpreted Hannah's desperate prayer and accused her of being drunk and showed little patience with her pain. Conversely, God knew her heart and heard her prayer.

Hannah somehow retained a good attitude throughout all her sorrow. An examination of her story reveals three important principles for the Christian to embrace. If implemented into our lives, these will serve as spiritual preventive maintenance to prevent temptation from overwhelming us.

Church Attendance

Hannah lived in a different age than we, and attendance at the principal place of Jewish worship was inconvenient at best. Due to the distance to the place of worship and since the concept of corporate worship was more male-focused, she could have conveniently stayed away from the house of worship. Instead, she continued to attend God's house. "Year by year...she went to the house of the Lord" (I Samuel 1:7). Of course, we're not advocating that annual church attendance at Christmas or Easter is sufficient for living a victorious Christian life; however, for Hannah the annual trip to the house of God was a task. She lived in the hill country, some twelve miles or so distance from the Jewish center of worship at that time, Shiloh. Undoubtedly, there were local spiritual gatherings for Hannah to attend, and religious teaching and devotion were part of her daily life. Still, Elkanah's family made the annual trip to offer a sacrifice at the tabernacle in Shiloh. It would have been understandable if Hannah had opted out of this rugged annual trek, but she did not.

In describing Hannah's attendance at the house of God, the Bible states, "...And the two sons of Eli, Hophni and Phinehas, the priests of the Lord, were there" (I Samuel 1:3). This seemingly irrelevant insertion serves to demonstrate Hannah's faithfulness. If anyone had a justifiable excuse for not going to God's house, Hannah did, for Hophni and Phinehas were very vile men (I Samuel 2:12-25). They stooped so low into debauchery as to commit adultery with the women who assembled at the tabernacle, possibly even making advances toward Hannah. Still, she did not allow this horrendous wickedness to prevent her from attending the house of God. Neither did she rise up in anger against Eli when he wrongly accused her, though she could have truthfully condemned his own sons.

Regular church attendance is essential for victorious Christian living. It is like going to a fuel station. Unfriendly attendants, unpleasant gasoline fumes, long waiting lines, and escalating prices do not keep us from regular visits to the service station. We still go back because we don't want to be stranded somewhere along the highway. Likewise, no matter what shortcomings or frustrations we may see in the local church, it is imperative to attend faithfully or else find another church with fewer flaws that believes and teaches the Bible.

Scripture admonishes us, "Not forsaking the assembling of ourselves together, as the manner of some is; but exhorting one another: and so much more, as ye see the day approaching" (Hebrews 10:25). This passage underscores the necessity of church attendance, which serves two important purposes: the individual believer receives spiritual strength for self and, in turn, is an inspiration to others who observe their faithfulness. I have seen these two principles at work on numerous occasions. One such account specifically comes to mind. A family had been wrongly accused of a horrendous crime. Instead of hiding out in embarrassment or supposing everyone at church assumed their guilt, they continued to remain faithful in their church attendance, even hosting special prayer meetings in their home. Not only did they receive strength to endure this long and grueling ordeal, their faithfulness inspired the congregation.

We must not be deceived, as some have, into thinking we receive sufficient spiritual food at home, with no need of attending church. We do need devotion at home, but we also need to attend church regularly. To refuse to do so is to disobey the Scriptures. Disobedience will hinder spiritual growth and can eventually kill spiritual life. It is unfortunate that, due to various reasons, some cannot attend church. For these it is incumbent upon the church to go to them and minister to their needs.

Those who are irregular in church attendance lose communication with the body of Christ and isolate themselves from any organized effort to evangelize their community. Any witnessing they do loses its impact since they have no close church family to provide fellowship and encouragement for a potential convert. The church, local and universal, is God's plan of organization for His people. Within the body of Christ—the church—God has placed the ministry and the gifts of the Spirit. Not only do these aid us in our present needs, but they also serve as preventive maintenance, sometimes steering us around the pitfalls of the adversary.

Prayer

Hannah prayed consistently. "And she was in bitterness of soul, and prayed unto the LORD, and wept sore. And it came to pass, as she continued praying before the Lord..." (I Samuel 1:10, 12). Hannah promised in her prayers, if God gave her a son, she would give him unto the Lord's work. Nine months later she gave birth. She believed this child was the result of prayer, thus she called him Samuel, meaning "asked of God." True to her promise, when the child was old enough, she gave him back to the Lord, to assist in the Lord's work. After delivering the child to the house of worship, Hannah continued to pray (I Samuel 2:1-10). She didn't perceive the magnitude of her prayers; they would prevent spiritual blindness in Israel and bring revival to the people.

Fast-forward the scene. Hannah's child grew up in the house of worship, but things didn't go well. The enemy captured the Ark of God, and Eli's sons died in the battle. Upon hearing the news, Eli fell from a chair and died of a broken neck. A distraught daughter-in-law went into labor, gave birth, and called Eli's grandson Ichabod (meaning "the glory is departed from Israel"). All seemed gloom

70

and despair, but Hannah's prayers were still alive. They were living in the heart of her young son, Samuel. This son, born of her prayers, was destined to turn Israel back to God. The preventive maintenance prayer of Hannah blessed an entire nation. Were it not for Hannah's prayer, Israel would not have had the great prophet and judge, Samuel, after the death of Eli.

At the request of His disciples, Jesus instructed them in praying (Luke 11). Significantly, this passage records only three verses on what to pray (Luke 11:2-4), but nine verses on encouragement to pray (Luke 11:5-13). Christ was not only interested in teaching us how to pray, but He also wanted to make certain that we do pray.

Jesus' model prayer included preventive maintenance: "Lead us not into temptation; but deliver us from evil" (Luke 11:4). "I pray not that thou shouldest take them out of the world, but that thou shouldest keep them from the evil. . .Neither pray I for these alone, but for them also which shall believe on me through their word" (John 17:15, 20). Doctor Harold Miller, a dear family friend, related this story of preventive prayer:

> "I was doctoring a girl who had already lost one child but who desperately wanted to have a baby. As a doctor, I sometimes become very emotionally involved with the patients, and such was the case in this situation. I considered prayer, but that seemed a little hypocritical since prayer was not part of my life. Many years before, I had concluded that science and religion were in conflict. I chose science, leaving behind the traditions of my parents. Out of desperation for this woman to have not only a child but a healthy child, I was prompted to do some talking with God. It had been a long time since I had prayed, but I did some serious talking with the Lord. I even made a deal. 'Lord, if you are truly God, please allow this woman to bear a healthy baby. If you do, I will make some changes in my way of life, especially in church attendance.'"

When the time for the delivery of the baby came, Doctor Miller was the physician's assistant in the delivery room. He explained what happened next:

> "I had not fully discussed my concerns with the specialist, so it was rather surprising when he turned to me and said, 'I think we should take the baby Caesarean.' He had no solid reason for this decision, only an intuition or inclination, or maybe a thought from heaven. Surgery was performed and the umbilical cord was found wrapped about the infant's neck. Had the child been born naturally, it would have died. I knew prayer had prevented its death."

Not only was the life of the child spared, but also faith abandoned in medical school was reborn in the heart of' Doctor Miller.

It's difficult for us to calculate the many problems, perils, and evils our prayers have prevented. We can be assured that preventive prayer is far better than a prayer for cure, for preventive prayer leaves no regrets or scars. We aren't always conscious for what we need to pray, but the Holy Spirit guides us in how we ought to pray. "Likewise the Spirit also helpeth our infirmities: for we know not what we should pray for as we ought: but the Spirit itself maketh intercession for us with groanings which cannot be uttered. And he that searcheth the hearts knoweth what is the mind of the Spirit, because he maketh intercession for the saints according to the will of God" (Romans 8:26-27). The eternal God, who sees the future, has established a means whereby we can prevent tragedies from happening. That means is prayer. To pray preventive maintenance prayers, we must pray biblically, which includes, "Seek the Lord and his strength, seek his face continually" (I Chronicles 16:11). We should pray often, fulfilling the Scripture, "Pray without ceasing" (I Thessalonians 5:17). Jesus taught, "…men ought always to pray, and not to faint" (Luke 18:1). He told the disciples, "Watch and pray, that ye enter not into temptation: the spirit indeed is willing, but the flesh is weak" (Matthew 26:41).

Preventive maintenance praying includes prayers not only for ourselves but also for others. "Praying always with all prayer and supplication in the Spirit, and watching there-unto with all persever-ance and supplication for all saints" (Ephesians 6:18). How reassur-ing it is when a fellow Christian says, "I felt impressed to pray for you." Only God knows what his prayers prevented.

A Sweet Spirit

Hannah kept a sweet spirit throughout her trials. She could have been hateful to Peninnah, who bore several children and reminded Hannah continually that she was barren; instead, she never retaliat-ed. The rebuke of Eli, the priest, and his accusation of drunkenness were enough to upset any decent woman, but Hannah did not fight back, nor did she become bitter. Hannah remained even-tempered. Though living in a house with the potential for constant strife, she remained peaceable.

Though favored by Elkanah above Peninnah, Hannah made no imperious demands such as Sarah made to Abraham regarding Hagar. Hannah remained agreeable in a disagreeable situation. Han-nah was unable to change this frustrating situation, but she did not permit the circumstances to make her bitter. This is not suggesting she accepted her plight passively; rather, she remained pleasant in the home, all the while expressing her anguish unto the Lord. When someone encounters trying circumstances and yet maintains an un-varyingly sweet spirit, there is the possibility of incredible triumph. For Hannah, the result was not only a son but also three other sons and two daughters. For Israel, the prevailing clouds of gloom were dispelled by the light of God that became brighter and brighter as the lad Samuel "grew before the Lord" (I Samuel 2:21).

The average person does not remain sweet, especially in the face of adversity. This includes many Christians. In fact, the guilt that follows temper tantrums keeps many of God's children from enjoying a more victorious life. It is possible, like Hannah, to remain a resilient believer in the midst of adverse conditions. Since Hannah lived prior to the completion of Scripture, we have a distinct advan-tage over her when facing problems. While her knowledge of God was restricted, we have an entire library of Scripture that records God's dealings with mankind.

How can we keep a sweet spirit? The key to experiencing peace in the midst of a tempest is knowing that God has everything under control. A regular diet of God's Word will build childlike faith in our hearts. We simply believe that God is in control of our lives.

We reject Murphy's Law: "What can go wrong, will go wrong." In contrast, nothing will go wrong that is beyond God's control. Things may look wrong to the carnal observer, but they are not. God does nothing wrong, and He will work all things together for our good (Romans 8:28). We may not always understand God's objectives, but we acknowledge that all circumstances undergo His scrutiny. And so we remain calm; we take no irrational action.

The psalmist stated, "I have not departed from thy judgments: for thou hast taught me. How sweet are thy words unto my taste! Yea, sweeter than honey to my mouth!" (Psalm 119:102-103). When we ingest the Word of God, though sometimes bitter to the flesh, it produces a sweet, tranquil spirit within us, which cannot help but transform our external actions.

Bible Reading

As the preceding verses indicate, to remain a healthy Christian, our spiritual diet must include the Word of God as well as prayer. Moses told Israel, "And he humbled thee, and suffered thee to hunger, and fed thee with manna, which thou knewest not, neither did thy fathers know; that he might make thee know that man doth not live by bread only, but by every word that proceedeth out of the mouth of the Lord doth man live" (Deuteronomy 8:3). Jesus used this verse to gain victory over Satan's temptations (Matthew 4:4). Likewise, Job expressed, "I have esteemed the words of his mouth more than my necessary food" (Job 23:12). Further, the psalmist gave us a key for avoiding sin: "Thy word have I hid in mine heart, that I might not sin against thee" (Psalm 119:11).

In his letter to the church, the Apostle Peter expressed the importance of' the Word of God to the believer: "As newborn babes, desire the sincere milk of the word, that ye may grow thereby" (I Peter 2:2). The Bible teaches we should progress into spiritual adulthood, but the process always incorporates God's Word as the staple diet for growth. Indeed, the Bible is spiritual "soul" food. It is no coincidence we need a consistent diet of the Word of God to overcome temptation. Just as the baby digests food and converts it into energy and physical strength, so also the written Word produces spiritual strength in the life of the reader.

A quality physical diet incorporates a wide range of food groups, not just eating what tastes good. Likewise, to receive full nourishment, we should read a wide range of Biblical subjects. Perhaps we are intrigued and prefer prophecy. Prophecy is good and meant to be studied, but we need a well-rounded diet of Scripture. Therefore, we should read Scripture on all subjects. The New Testament writer admonishes, "Let us go on unto perfection" (Hebrews 6:1). To fulfill such a command necessitates extensive Bible knowledge. We should read from the entire Bible, both Old and New Testaments. We should read for doctrine, for inspiration, for comfort, and for correction. It is particularly beneficial to follow an organized plan of reading from the entire Bible and to continue this pattern consistently.

Both prayer and Bible reading are of utmost importance. The Scriptures teach us how to live, and they proclaim victory for us if we endure. Prayer enhances our strength to be obedient to the Scriptures. Failure to pray and study the Bible consistently leaves a Christian spiritually weak.

I've never forgotten an experiential lesson taught by my fourth grade teacher. As a class, we participated in an experiment that vividly illustrates the principle of a healthy diet. During the school year, our teacher kept two white mice in separate cages in our classroom. Daily we fed one mouse a well-balanced diet of what our teacher described as nutritional food. Likewise, we fed the other mouse, but we fed it junk food, or to be honest, we fed it the foodstuff we most enjoyed: candy, chips, and cake. The first mouse grew beautiful white fur and remained very playful. The second mouse, the junk-food mouse, seemed to enjoy eating as much as the other, but it grew weaker and uglier, losing the white, fur coat. If this experiment had continued further, I believe the mouse would have surely died before our eyes.

My dad was eighteen when he joined the navy and was assigned aboard the U.S.S. North Carolina. During World War II, this enormous and powerful battleship operated in the Pacific. In the midst of a heated battle, the billowing smoke from the 16-inch guns of the ship became so dense that the accompanying ships thought she had taken a direct hit. Only after the smoke had cleared could the rest of the fleet see that the Carolina was still afloat, still proudly fly-ing the U.S. flag. Such is the case with the Bible-reading, Bible-be-lieving Christian. In the heat of the battle, while some question and doubt, the believer waits, praying and reading God's Word. When the smoke settles, the flag of joyous victory is still waving.

These four disciplines—church attendance, daily prayer, main-taining a sweet spirit, and consistent Bible reading—serve as pre-ventive measures in the war against temptation. As protective armor, they shield us against the darts of Satan. The wise Christian includes these disciplines daily; therefore, they serve as preventive mainte-nance, sometimes allowing the believer to avoid certain temptations but certainly offering help in the midst of battle.

It seems prudent for a government to not wait for the enemy to attack before it builds an army of defense; it considers its best defense to be a good offense. The army is recruited, trained, and stands ready at all times to repel the slightest advance of the enemy. Likewise, these preventive acts of spiritual warfare on the part of the believer serve as an excellent offensive against temptation.

Points of Discussion

Share a personal tragedy that may have been prevented by applying spiritual preventive maintenance.

Which of the four preventive maintenance disciplines is least active in your life? How may you improve this discipline?

Discuss an area of your life that is similar to Hannah's. How are you applying the spiritual disciplines to overcome that trial?

CHAPTER 8

God's Fire Escape

Jim was thoroughly trained in the ancient martial arts, and his hands were rightly considered deadly weapons. Such abilities seemed worthless to a factory laborer whose job consisted of routine assembly work, but an opportunity to use them presented itself to Jim. Like a caged animal, Jim found himself taunted by a fellow worker. This verbal harassment continued for months, day after day. On most days, his disciplined lifestyle proved the harassment as child's play, but a few times an urge to prove his abilities seemed nearly overpowering. Such was the case on a very trying day. He was in no mood to be provoked by anyone, especially by a wimpish co-worker.

As so often before, Jim's fellow worker shot forth a flurry of barbed arrows of condescension. Jim's focus instantly narrowed, surveying his adversary. Hands and limbs snapped into trained position. His mind quickly issued the command to attack. A deathblow started its lightning movement. Death to his opponent would be sudden and sure, but in a split second's thought, Jim was able to halt his blow. To the astonishment of those watching, he turned quickly from his opponent and fled the building.

Jim's family had been praying for him to receive salvation, and that day God miraculously answered their prayers. His fellow workers didn't know it, but Jim went directly to the church to pray and give his life to Christ. This beautiful testimony of conversion illustrates a paradoxical truth: A means of escape always exists in the midst of a temptation designed to defeat us. "...God...will with the temptation also make a way to escape" (I Corinthians 10:13). Often, the way to escape is literally to flee the tempting situation. After promising guaranteed escape, Paul continued, "Wherefore my dearly beloved, flee from idolatry" (I Corinthians 10:14). The best way to overcome some temptations is by flight. This is God's escape plan from the fiery trials. When it seems impossible to overcome a temptation, there is still a door of escape: we can run from the temptation.

The military general who does not plan for a possible retreat may well find his army trapped by the enemy. The Christian who finds himself vulnerable to a temptation but does not flee the temptation by literally exiting the location may well be ensnared by it. It is impossible to prevent all temptations.

God has not commissioned us to prevent but to overcome. He has, however, promised a door of escape from every temptation. Nevertheless, some Christians fall prey to temptation needlessly by their unwillingness to use the one door of escape: flight. Because of their unwillingness to flee, their resolve to overcome is weakened. Day by day they become more vulnerable.

Here are three W's for using "God's fire escape" to exit temptation:

WHEN? Anytime a Christian is confronted by a temptation that seems greater than his ability to overcome, he should flee.

WHAT? When one is feeling vulnerable, he must literally flee the situation. He should simply get up and exit the very location of the temptation. A warning sign of vulnerability is the inner sense of pleasure from the temptation and a desire to facilitate the situation instead of preventing it.

WHERE? After the tempted has left the immediate danger, he should seek a place of safety from the immediate temptation. Find a place to be alone with God in prayer. If the vulnerability exists (perhaps you are forced back into the situation because it is your place of employment), you need to confide in someone who can help you choose from options for overcoming the temptation, join with you in prayer, and give continued guidance until the temptation is either conquered or removed. Jim, the young man mentioned earlier in this chapter, did exactly that; he ran to the church for guidance.

Most temptations are uninvited intruders. We do not seek them or do anything to encourage them; rather, they seek us, often to our surprise. Where do such temptations come from? Often they are suggestions from evil surroundings (billboards, co-workers, media, neighbors, enemies, sinners). Sometimes they are direct attacks from Satan's kingdom. Other times they arise from natural desires but in an unlawful or in a sinful means of fulfilling the desire. Like the wind, they can blow in unexpectedly. They can pop into the mind without warning. We don't have to seek sin, for it finds us. We cannot prevent the printing of obscene books and magazines, nor can we control the places and manner in which they are placed. A needed trip to the grocery store can find one confronted with the decision to gaze upon or turn the head from pornography. The producers of billboards do not ask our consent for the type of advertisement they display. All these serve as temptations designed to lure and ensnare us through the desires of the flesh. Satan takes natural desires and twists them into sinful temptations.

We cannot prevent these evils from existing. There is no temptation-free bubble into which we can cocoon ourselves until Jesus' return. A person can prevent some temptations simply by avoiding ungodly situations, but other times this is absolutely impossible. Most situations of temptation are out of our control. We must simply become overcomers. A man cannot control the sensual style of a woman's dress, but he does not have to look twice at an immodestly clothed woman. After realizing such a situation exists, he is free to look another direction. If he refuses to do so, he exposes his eyes to sinful pleasure and his heart to sinful desires. The end result of unleashed lust is adultery, either with the act or with intent.

A few years ago we were bombarded by a popular saying: "The devil made me do it." This statement attempted to evade personal responsibility for sin. The devil, however, is not directly responsible for all temptations, and he certainly is not responsible when we choose to sin. We may blame him or someone else for the temptation, but we are responsible for our actions toward the temptation. Some temptations become sins because we fail to use a God-given option to combat temptation: flight.

Eve did not invite the serpent into her home; he came to her. The suggestion for David to number Israel came directly from Satan. After Jesus had fasted, the tempter came to Him. These were all involuntary temptations. The individuals involved had to contend with an intruder. The cases of Lot, Samson, and Solomon are different in that each one voluntarily entered into temptation. Lot "pitched his tents toward Sodom" (Genesis 13:12). He chose his direction, and eventually he moved into Sodom. The Scripture is clear regarding Samson's failure. "Samson went down to Timnath, and saw a woman in Timnath of the daughters of the Philistines" (Judges 14:1). Against the wishes and instruction of his parents, Samson sought the love of heathen women, and one of them later betrayed and destroyed him. The allurement of evil women did not stop until Samson awoke out of sleep, with his head resting on the knees of Delilah. Sensing the danger he flexed his muscles as before and prepared to defend himself, only to find that God's Spirit had departed. He was unwilling to flee sin but assumed sin would never conquer him. Unfortunately, and contrary to the theology of some meaningful teachers, God's Spirit doesn't dwell indefinitely with one who willfully chooses to remain in a place of carnality. Because Samson refused to flee the evil companionship of the Philistines, God's Spirit departed from him, leaving him powerless in the midst of his adversaries. Similarly, because Solomon (though the wisest of men), contrary to the commands of Scripture, married heathen wives, he forsook his monotheistic faith. "Solomon went after Ashtoreth the goddess of" the Zidonians, and after Milcom the abomination of the Ammonites" (I Kings 11:5). Instead of following the commands of Scripture, he chose the traditions of kings in marrying into alliances. His associations with idolatrous wives caused him to be overtaken by idolatry. The wisest man did not learn the simple principle of fleeing temptation. Solomon knew what to do, but this great teacher did not apply his lessons to his own life.

Solomon, in his wisdom to others, related the story of a young man who was seduced into adultery by a harlot. The story plainly illustrates the consequences of deliberately walking into temptation and not fleeing from it. With the wisdom of the ancients and with the love of a father, he writes:

> For at the window of my house I looked through my casement, and beheld among the simple ones, I discerned among the youths, a young man void of understanding, passing through the street near her corner; and he went the way to her house. In the twilight, in the evening, in the black and dark night: And, behold, there met him a woman with the attire of an harlot, and subtil of heart. (She is loud and stubborn; her feet abide not in her house: Now is she without, now in the streets, and lieth in wait at every corner.) So she caught him, and kissed him, and with an impudent face [spoke] unto him. . .With her much fair speech she caused him to yield, with the flattering of her lips she forced him. He goeth after her straightway, as an ox goeth to the slaughter, or as a fool to the correction of the stocks; Till a dart strike through his liver; as a bird hasteth to the snare, and knoweth not that it is for his life.
>
> Proverbs 7:6-13, 21-23

To his younger disciple Timothy, Paul wrote, "Flee also youthful lusts" (II Timothy 2:22). Knowing well that many worldly allurements could beset and even overcome Timothy, Paul straightforwardly admonished him to flee: to actively avoid temptations that appealed to immature and fleshly desires.

Voluntary exposure to temptation does not necessarily produce strength. To the contrary, it often works as a conditioning process to dilute one's perspective regarding sin, and it diminishes one's resolve to overcome. A person becomes so accustomed to the tempting situation that he no longer views it as dangerous or as sinful. His convictions diminish until he can partake without feeling condemnation. Alexander Pope expressed this conditioning process: "Vice is a monster of so frightful mien, As to be hated needs but to be seen; Yet seen too oft, familiar her face, We first endure, then pity, then embrace."[15]

Israel drifted into a state of spiritual insensitivity to God's moral laws. She no longer felt shame or blushed when she committed abominations. The prophet lamented, "Were they ashamed when they had committed abomination? nay, they were not at all ashamed, neither could they blush: therefore they shall fall among them that fall: at the time that I visit them they shall be cast down, saith the LORD" (Jeremiah 6:15). Likewise, when we compare yesteryear's lifestyles with that of today's society, many view common decency as a bit old-fashioned. Exposure to immorality can certainly soften the repulsiveness of sin. Our spiritual default mode is not necessarily righteousness; contrariwise, an unchecked flesh drifts toward carnality.

King David's first glimpse of Bathsheba may have been innocent, but his continued gaze to gratify his eyes with her beauty and nakedness, refusing to turn his head as she bathed, resulted not only in lust but an uncontrolled desire to have her. His refusal to turn his head and walk away from the balcony overlooking her patio sparked a natural desire that soon turned into a burning lust. Prolonged contemplation of improper desire resulted in justification of his actions. He became calloused to condemnation. "After all," he probably reasoned, "I am King of Israel, and the king is lord of his subjects and should not be denied his desires." A tragic event followed, causing needless harm to many. The results were felt from the palace to the battlefield. A loyal soldier in David's army died senselessly because of David's sins. A longstanding friendship was severed between Bathsheba's grandfather (who was David's royal advisor) and David. David's sin affected lives from Jerusalem all the way to Egypt, where a rebellious son was exiled. From those distant times until now, when Sunday school boys are saddened by the failure of their giant killing hero, we've felt the sting of sin. A turn of the head could have prevented all of this.

God created us with certain natural desires, but these desires do not automatically regulate themselves. Each individual must learn to control them. Because of the fallen Adamic nature, our desires know few boundaries. We must determine limitations for them, guided by the Word and Spirit of God. Moreover, never in this life can we honestly say, "I have conquered my natural desires permanently and completely."

For a natural desire to be conquered permanently, a physical change has to occur. Sometimes, physical illness or disease can destroy a person's appetite or sexual desires. Unless this happens, natural appetites and desires will remain. Our responsibility is to control them. Since the devil understands man's physical makeup, he has launched an attack to encourage the uncontrolled, undisciplined exercise of our natural desires.

These natural desires are not something we should seek to destroy but something we must control. One of the best ways to exercise control is to avoid situations that tempt us to allow natural desires to be acted out against God's righteous plan. In order to keep these natural desires in a righteous setting, flight is "God's fire escape" for many temptations. As an example, a person who finds it difficult to abstain from alcohol should not go to places where he would be tempted to drink. Likewise, if someone has difficulty in breaking the habit of illicit drugs, he should not associate with those who would encourage him to do drugs. Dating couples should avoid situations conducive to excessive bodily contact which leads to lust. A housewife who wonders if she is still attractive and desirable to her husband should not clutter her mind with romance novels that would suggest an extramarital affair.

We can best deal with some temptations by avoidance. Paul wrote, "Abstain from all appearance of evil" (I Thessalonians 5:22). Jesus taught in his model prayer, "Lead us not into temptation" (Matthew 6:18). We bear much of the responsibility for making that prayer a reality. God's fire escape is available for the untamed temptations. To reject His way of escape is spiritual suicide.

Points of Discussion

Discuss God's fire escape from temptation.

Discuss a time when you needed to use this fire escape.

Discuss ways in which we voluntary enter into temptation.

How do natural desires create temptation, and what actions can you take to prevent natural desires from causing you to commit sin?

CHAPTER 9

Early Warning System

O f major importance in today's defense system is an early alarm system commonly called "radar." Radar is a coined word from letters of the phrase "radio detecting and ranging." The system not only detects the existence of an incoming object but also reveals its location and speed of flight. This gives the operator advance warning of an attack, and such information provides the opportunity to intercept the intruder and repel his attack.

Today's intelligence satellites can monitor enemy movements worldwide. From technology circling the globe thousands of miles above the earth, technicians hunched over computers on ships and land bases are able to intercept and decode telephone conversations flashed around the world by microwave. Such eavesdropping is routine and essential for the protection of our country against potential enemies. To curtail this continual surveillance would be to relinquish our freedom.

December 7, 1941, 7:55 A.M. marked the beginning of a massive air assault of Pearl Harbor. Little more than one hour later, after inflicting heavy casualties on the U.S. forces, the invaders withdrew.

Combined U.S. Navy and Army fatalities totaled over 2,200, and in addition to the loss of lives, numerous ships and planes were destroyed. The invading forces escaped without being attacked. Although we do not know the full story of the defense of Pearl Harbor, history bears record that the incident did not happen without some warning, which, if properly interpreted and acted upon, might have prevented the devastation on that fatal December morning. According to accepted history, on that morning an army private, practicing on a radar set, detected a large flight of approaching planes. His lieutenant told him to dismiss the idea of invasion since they were expecting a flight of B-17's from the mainland. Could this detection, if properly acted upon, have enabled the U.S. to repel the Japanese assault? Perhaps it could even have prevented the prolonged war in the Pacific? It is possible American soldiers—some we know personally—would not have experienced the horrors of the Bataan Death March. If someone had acted properly upon this early warning, it is conceivable that my own father and many others would not have experienced the atrocities of the war.

God has, likewise, given us an early warning system to use against Satan's attacks. For us to ignore the warnings and to fail to prepare a counterattack may mean total defeat. We should not take these warnings lightly but should give them our immediate attention. To hesitate can be disastrous.

Numerous times throughout the Bible, God's warnings preceded Satan's attacks. Such a warning, if heeded, could have prevented the first murder. "And the LORD said unto Cain, Why art thou wroth? and why is thy countenance fallen? If thou doest well, shalt thou not be accepted? and if thou doest not well, sin lieth at the door. And unto thee shall be his desire, and thou shalt rule over him" (Genesis 4:6-7). To Balaam God warned, "Thou shalt not go with them" (Numbers 22:12). Even though Balaam did not heed God's first warning, other warnings followed. A warrior angel of the Lord stood in the way, and the donkey turned aside from the path three times, the third time crushing Balaam's foot against a wall. Still, Balaam persisted in his personal ambition, neglecting the warning of the Lord. Finally, "God opened the mouth of the ass, and she said unto Balaam, What have I done unto thee, that thou hast smitten me these three times?" (Numbers 22:28). Balaam was so impervious to

God's will that he was unable to see what the donkey saw all along: an angel of the Lord with a drawn sword. In His mercy, God allowed Balaam to see the angel. Both Cain and Balaam failed to heed these early warnings. Needless to say, both miserably failed God.

Throughout the Old Testament, the prophets of God gave numerous warnings to the people. When the people heeded and acted upon the warnings, the Lord averted the impending danger. When the people rejected the warnings, they suffered defeat.

What is the early warning system that can help us detect the attacks of Satan? There are three primary ways in which God warns us of temptations to come.

The Word of God

The Bible, when read and applied, is a constant alarm system that identifies the enemy's attempts to invade our lives. Paul, referring to the scriptural accounts of Israel's failures, explained, "They are written for our admonition" (I Corinthians 10:11). Just as ignorance of the law of the land is no excuse for illegal activities, so ignorance of the Bible is no excuse for sin, especially for a Christian. However, the new believer is not judged according to the Christian who has an abundant knowledge of Scripture. Still, one who has received Christ should immediately become a student of Scripture.

Through the centuries Bible translators have meticulously recorded and preserved the Scripture, making it possible for us to know the will of God. It allows us to readily identify a temptation. It leaves no question as to what we should do. Our knowledge of Scripture will automatically trigger an early warning and defense system.

Paul urged, "Be not conformed to this world: but be ye transformed by the renewing of your mind, that ye may prove what is that good, and acceptable, and perfect, will of God" (Romans 12:2). We renew our minds through exposure to a thorough knowledge of God's Word. The Psalmist explained, "Thy word have I hid in mine heart, that I might not sin against thee" (Psalm 119:11).

A radar system is useless when unmonitored. Its warnings are of no avail if no one is there to observe. Likewise, the Bible, if not consistently read, will be of little value in warning the believer of Satan's attacks. The Bible admonishes us to be vigilant, or watchful of our enemy (I Peter 5:8), and assures us that we do not have to be ignorant of his deception (II Corinthians 2:11). How do we recognize him? The Bible is our radar screen. Temptation cannot elude its detection.

Though we're unsure who penned the words, the author expressed these thoughts about the Bible in a succinct manner: "This book contains the mind of God, the state of man, the doom of sinners, the happiness of believers. Read it to be wise, believe it to be safe, and practice it to be holy. It contains light to direct you, food to support you and comfort to cheer you. Christ is its grand object, our good its design and the glory of God its end."[16] Daily Bible reading should be a consistent part of our schedule. Its message will sound forth alarms in our lives, enabling us to evade temptation or to meet and defeat temptation.

God's Anointed Ministry

Preaching the gospel is much more than a profession; it is a divine calling. The preacher stands as God's mouthpiece to direct us in God's will. The Holy Spirit that anointed the writers of Scripture also anoints the ministry who share God's Word through sermons. The pastor is a vital link between us and heaven. One of the duties of the ministry is to warn God's people. This is not an optional responsibility, nor is it always pleasurable for him.

The prophet of Scripture explained the responsibility of ministry when he wrote, "Son of' man, I have made thee a watchman unto the house of Israel: therefore, hear the word at my mouth, and give them warning from me" (Ezekiel 3:17). Further, he warned the ministry, "…but if the watchman see the sword come, and blow not the trumpet, and the people be not warned; if the sword come, and take any person from among them, he is taken away in his iniquity; but his blood will I require at the watchman's hand" (Ezekiel 33:6).

Just as the preacher's obligation is to warn, so the believer's responsibility is to obey and submit. The Scripture teaches, "Obey them that have the rule over you, and submit yourselves: for they watch for your souls" (Hebrews 13:17). When this scriptural concept is in focus, a beautiful harmony prevails in the church. Paul combined both the ministry and laity responsibility toward Scripture when he wrote, "And he gave some, apostles; and some, prophets; and some, evangelists; and some, pastors and teachers; For the perfecting of the saints, for the work of the ministry, for the edifying of the body of Christ" (Ephesians 4:11-12). Verse twelve's punctuation of a comma separating saints and ministry was not present in the original Greek but was supplied by the King James translators. This simple comma may lead one to assume these five offices of ministry are given for three separate tasks of the ministry: equipping the saints; the work of ministry; edifying the believers. The verse actually means, however, that these five offices are given to perfect or equip the saints, so that the saints can perform the ministry or service of the church, so that the entire body of believers can be more effectively ministered to, rather than a pastor or pastoral staff having to minister to the needs of each individual. The New King James Version clarifies, "For the equipping of the saints for the work of ministry, for the edifying of the body of Christ" (Ephesians 4:12 NKJV).

The pastor's responsibility is to train the saints for their ministry (service). When the pastor gives godly instruction, he is not trying to dominate people's lives but is simply obeying God's command. For God's purpose to be accomplished to the potential, the saints must respond in obedience and submission. When the pastor preaches God's Word, he preaches out of obligation to God. When we hear such a message, it is our obligation to obey. Obedience to God's Word is not optional; it is essential to salvation. To ignore a biblical message is to turn off the alarm system. The enemy's attack will inevitably come.

The Spirit of God

One of the works of the Holy Spirit is guidance. There are times when we must seek direction directly from the promptings of God's Spirit. This leadership will never contradict the written Word nor does it replace the authority of spiritual leaders. Rather, it provides additional help in our battle against Satan's deception.

Jesus spoke of the coming Spirit as a guide: "Howbeit when he, the Spirit of truth, is come, he will guide you into all truth: for he shall not speak of himself; but whatsoever he shall hear, that shall he speak: and he will shew you things to come" (John 16:13). The Spirit directed Peter to preach to Cornelius (Acts 10:19-20), and thus was brought into the first church Gentile believers. For some reason unknown to us, the Spirit redirected Paul from journeying east into Asia; instead, the Spirit directed him to travel toward the west (Acts 16:6).

The indwelling Spirit can serve as an early warning system of the attack of Satan. Thus, we should not take lightly the Spirit's prompting. God may be warning us of approaching temptation.

The Spirit may warn us to avoid a dangerous or questionable situation or may encourage us in certain beneficial activities. This prompting of the Spirit will often come as an urging to pray. It may come in the middle of the night. When this happens we should be sensitive to the Spirit and obey the prompting. By doing so we may avert tragedy in our lives or in the lives of others. Jesus told Simon Peter, "Satan hath desired to have you...but I have prayed for thee" (Luke 22:31-32).

The Holy Spirit can speak to us in various ways. If we are sensitive to His promptings, we can avoid spiritual tragedy. Just as a smoke alarm detects the presence of fire and sends out a warning, so the Holy Spirit detects and warns of impending spiritual danger.

Our Spiritual Iron Dome Defense System

The nation of Israel, with assistance from the United States, developed what is commonly called an iron dome defense system that protects against missiles launched into their country by their enemy. An arrangement of highly sophisticated defensive batteries are scattered throughout Israel. Each battery has three necessary components that operate in sequence: a radar detection unit that picks up the launch of a missile toward their country; a management center that predicts where the missile will land and determines whether it should be intercepted; a launcher that fires an interceptor missile at the incoming enemy projectile and destroys it in midair. Likewise, God has given us, through His Word, a spiritual iron dome defense system. The system is simple, yet effective: "In every thing give thanks" (I Thessalonians 5:18).

Paul wrote these words to the church he established in Thessalonica. During Paul's day, it was a city of about two hundred thousand people, with a large Jewish community. During his second missionary journey, he spent three Sabbaths in the city, sharing the Gospel in the streets and in the synagogue. The result was the conversion of some Jews and many Gentiles. Some Jewish non-believers stirred up the community against Paul and his fellow laborer Silas. The persecution was so severe that the Thessalonian believers, fearing for their safety, sent them away under the protection of the night.

Because Paul was forced to leave this young church so abruptly, he sent them a letter to offer direction in their newfound faith. Included in the letter are a number of instructions. This verse is one of those instructions. The directive, "in everything give thanks," is a difficult verse to obey, for it goes against human nature and takes much effort. The command was given without qualification: give thanks for the good and the bad. But why should we give thanks for all things? First, the instruction was not to give thanks "for" all things; rather, we are to give thanks "in" all things.

Why give thanks during all things, especially difficult situations? It is a spiritual act on the part of the believer, combining both faith and obedience. It acknowledges God's goodness even though you can't see, hear, or feel His presence.

Giving thanks during times of adversity is a spiritual principle which doesn't necessarily make sense to mankind—neither does turning the other cheek, preferring your brother, or the Christian receiving life because Christ died. The principle works accordingly: we give thanks to God regardless of how we feel, and He gives us joy in spite of our circumstances.

A thankful heart becomes our spiritual dome of defense. Like the physical iron dome of defense protecting Israel, this spiritual dome has three components. First, thankfulness acts as a form of protection. A thankful heart opens the heart of the believer to God's continual presence. Nothing can penetrate God's shield without His permission.

Second, thankfulness opens our minds to God's thoughts: Under any circumstances, when we think God thoughts, our problems diminish. God thoughts are bigger than our problems. When we spend time giving God thanks, and we are absorbed with God thoughts, there is little time left to worry. Paul explained to his associate Timothy how a thankful heart, though in the midst of trouble, contributed to his victorious living: "For the which cause I also suffer these things: nevertheless I am not ashamed: for I know whom I have believed, and am persuaded that he is able to keep that which I have committed unto him against that day" (II Timothy 1:12).

Finally, thankfulness opens our emotions to God's peace: "And the peace of God, which passeth all understanding, shall keep your hearts and minds through Christ Jesus" (Philippians 4:7). Thankfulness becomes a weapon to which Satan has no counteraction, for when he sends his best shot, and you say "thanks God," he doesn't know what else to do. As long as you complain, protest, grumble, criticize, whine, and pout, Satan keeps firing his missiles of destruction. When we start giving thanks, we create a spiritual dome of defense that Satan cannot penetrate.

Points of Discussion

Which of the early warning disciplines is least active in your life? Why?

How may you facilitate the early warning system in your life?

Thinking back to a failure in your life, was there a warning you failed to heed?

Discuss the concept of giving God thanks for everything—including the difficult—as producing a spiritual shield against the attacks of Satan.

CHAPTER 10

What Should A Christian Who Has Sinned Do?

S atan says there is no hope for the Christian who has sinned. "You are doomed to burn on the trash heap along with millions of others who have failed God," he sneers. This is simply not true. There are actually three roads from which the Christian who has sinned can choose: the road of the backslider, the road of the hypocrite, or the road of repentance. None of the three are easy roads to travel, but eternal destiny depends on the choice made. Only the road of repentance will lead to eternal salvation; the other two lead to inevitable destruction.

The Road of the Backslider

Every Christian is potentially a backslider. A backslider is not just the former deacon who is now the town drunk. A backslider is any Christian who stops progressing in the will of God and starts regressing into the world of sin. The path to heaven is an uphill climb; conversely, the path to eternal damnation is a slippery slope. We are either climbing upward or sliding backward. Coasting into heaven is impossible.

We should never boast of personal spiritual prowess but should realize that only by the grace of God can we prevail against sin. Many spiritual giants have miserably failed God: Adam the first, Moses the meekest, Samson the strongest, David the beloved, Solomon the wisest, Peter the chosen, and Demas the missionary. We could add many great men of our own generation to this list. Such a repertoire of the failed and fallen teaches us to take heed lest we, too, should fall and become castaways.

In a case study of backsliders, there are at least three stages in the journey of a backslider. The obvious sinful lifestyle is not the first step of regression from saint to sinner; rather, sin is the result of a backsliding path that is taken prior to committing sin. The committing of sin is the end result of a chosen path away from the disciplined Christian lifestyle.

Lukewarmness is the first stage of backsliding. The only prophetic book of the New Testament describes lukewarmness as, "...neither cold nor hot" (Revelation 3:15). It's an in-between state. In this status one's life is not consciously given over to the world, but any commitment to the Lord is shaky at best. This initial stage is usually characterized not by sins of commission but rather by sins of omission. These sins may include lack of personal prayer and Bible reading or inconsistency in Christian disciplines such as church attendance and personal ministry. At this stage the person is often too busy with personal responsibilities to be involved in accountabilities to Christ and the local church. One often omits Christian disciplines long before committing sin. Jesus described this stage in the parable of the ten virgins (Matthew 25:1-13). In the parable, five virgins were wise and kept enough oil in their lamps. These can be classified as observing Christian disciplines. Five of the virgins were foolish and failed to keep oil in their lamps. The five foolish virgins exemplify the lukewarm stage of the backslider: they haven't sold out to the world, they still attend church with some measure of expectation, and they have a certain resemblance of Christianity. When a situation arises that requires strength to overcome, the lukewarm Christian is unprepared and lacks sufficient strength to combat the adversary. Christ passed judgment upon this lukewarm condition: "So then because thou art lukewarm, and neither cold nor hot, I will spue thee out of my mouth" (Revelation 3:16). The lukewarm Christian, one who has experienced the love and grace of Calvary but no longer appreciates it, operates apart from God's favor. Unless one who is lukewarm repents and changes the lifestyle that has brought on this condition, he is in danger of two consequences. He may well slip into the second stage of the backslider—sins of commission, or worse still, as previously stated, God warned that He may sever the relationship (Revelation 3:16).

Since lukewarmness operates apart from basic Christian disciplines, this state leads to committing sinful acts. The lukewarm individual doesn't necessarily dive into sin. At first these sins may be subtle: passionless worship of Christ, grudgingly giving the tithe and offerings, fault finding toward the body of Christ, crossing lines of discreteness. Since the Holy Spirit prompting detects and reveals such acts, but the lukewarm person is somewhat insensitive to the Holy Spirit, or at best slow to respond, the lukewarm live in constant danger of returning to the world of sin. In both the first stage (lukewarmness) and second stage (returning to the world of sin) there is hope: repentance. God's Spirit still draws the backslider. It is possible for him to recognize his backslidden state, repent of his sins, and be restored to favor with God. However, to continue on the path of the backslider there are two grave dangers. One, there is the danger of drifting into the third stage—in which there is little hope of recovery. Two, the backslider lives in the ever-present possibility of dying, thus facing eternal judgment—from which the backslider has no hope.

Apostasy is the before mentioned possible third stage of the backslider. At this stage the backslider rejects righteousness, denies the truth of Scripture, and rejects God's Spirit to such an extent that God becomes irrelevant in his life. At this stage God releases the backslider to follow sin and Satan. The apostate is totally defenseless against a savage devil and is totally exposed to the power of Satan, including Satan's most deadly weapon: the lie. "And for this cause God shall send them strong delusion, that they should believe a lie: that they all might be damned who believed not the truth, but had pleasure in unrighteousness" (II Thessalonians 2:11-12). Spiritual blindness pervades his life. The apostate, void of truth, is absent of the protecting armor of God's love. The outcome? He is vulnerable to satanic deception. Satan's lie is so convincing that the apostate believes it and is totally deceived. Consequently, he will never change his lifestyle and will be eternally lost.

The backslider thinks irrationally. He forsakes a loving Savior for a malicious devil. He trades eternal hope for endless torment in the lake of fire. He gives up a pure conscience for nagging guilt. He exchanges white garments for filthy rags. He swaps his royal birthright to become a child of a fallen angel. Like Esau of old, he peddles the favor of God for a bowl of soup. He is the most foolish among fools.

The Road of the Hypocrite

No Christian has never sinned. The danger in failure is failing to admit the failure, declining grace, and acting as if everything is fine. When we fail, if we do nothing about failure and continue to act as if we have never sinned, we may end up on the road of the hypocrite.

The road of hypocrisy runs parallel with that of the apostate. The apostate denies that there is sin; the hypocrite hides his sin. Just as the apostate is hopeless because he cannot accept the grace of God, likewise, the hypocrite is without God's saving grace as long as he continues his life of pretense and denial of sin. "For what is the hope of the hypocrite, though he hath gained, when God taketh away his soul?" (Job 27:8).

The fangs of guilt eat away at the hypocrite's heart. The fear of discovery haunts each conscious moment. His peace of mind is destroyed. The hypocrite cannot enjoy singing in the choir or teaching a Sunday school class. The hypocrite fakes God's grace while living apart from God's favor. Unlike the apostate, the hypocrite knows right from wrong, but like the apostate, he is in danger of believing a lie from the devil, deceiving himself about his spiritual condition, and may cut himself off from God's grace.

The Road to Repentance

The third road is that of repentance. Repentance includes an acknowledgment of guilt and a request for forgiveness. The Scripture guarantees forgiveness to the repentant Christian. "If we confess our sins, he is faithful and just to forgive us our sins, and to cleanse us from all unrighteousness" (I John 1:9). John wrote these words to the saints, not to the unregenerate. He included himself in the passage by using the pronoun we. Likewise, we should place ourselves in this passage and claim its promise for each of us individually. If we sin, we must confess our sins to the Lord. Once we confess to the Lord, He will forgive us.

John wasn't suggesting we live carelessly, sinning at will every day. To the contrary, he exhorted, "These things write I unto you, that ye sin not" (I John 2:1). At the same time, John warned us against a self-righteous attitude of "I never sin." He cautioned, "If we say that we have not sinned, we make him a liar, and his word is not in us" (I John 1:10). Hopefully, we stop lying and avoid committing acts of lust and greed. The Holy Spirit within and the laws of the land without motivate us to stop stealing and to refrain from killing. Still, the subtle sins of the flesh often trip us up: thoughts, motives, and emotions. Jesus challenged these invisible sins when He said, "Ye have heard that it was said by them of old time, Thou shalt not commit adultery: But I say unto you, That whosoever looketh on a woman to lust after her hath committed adultery with her already in his heart" (Matthew 5:27-28).

Though sins of the heart are not viewed as being as bad as outward sins, we have all failed in these areas since we were saved. All sins must be dealt with. We have the Biblical plan to deal with sin: confession to Christ of any and all sin. At that point of confession (We generally refer to this act as repentance.), Jesus Christ's blood covers our sins. What a wonderful privilege! Without this promise, all of us would be without hope.

Someone may lament, "I have confessed that sin many times, but I still feel guilty for my sin." Confessing twice for a singular act of sin is once too many. One sincere, repentant confession brings forgiveness. If you commit the sin again, you should confess again, but once you have confessed, you should accept Christ's forgiveness through faith. Further, use your energy to avoid committing the same sin again instead of using your energy feeling guilty.

If you have sin in your life that you have not confessed, you should confess it now. If you have confessed the sin but still feel guilty, you should verbally acknowledge forgiveness now. "Lord Jesus, I thank You for Calvary and that Your horrendous death has covered by debt of sin. I accept Your sacrifice for my sins." Once you have truly repented, your sin is forgiven. Whether you feel forgiven or not, God's Word is true. You must accept forgiveness by faith.

Sanctification by the Spirit

The repented Christian can live a life of sanctification (separation unto the Lord; separation from sin) by the power of the indwelling Holy Spirit. Receiving the Holy Spirit is an essential part of the new birth experience. It is essential, first of all, because Christ commanded it. "Jesus answered, Verily, verily, I say unto thee, Except a man be born of water and of the Spirit, he cannot enter into the kingdom of God" (John 4:5). The Holy Spirit baptism is the only way in which Christ lives within us. One should not settle for the traditional invitational prayer where he invites Christ into his heart; one should experience the Holy Spirit infilling: Acts 2:1-4; Acts 8:15-17; Acts 10:44-46; Acts 19:6.

Receiving the Spirit is also essential so the believer can be an overcomer of sin. Christ's Spirit within us counteracts both external and internal temptations. The new birth does not eliminate temptations, but, as Spirit-filled believers, we are no longer held in bondage by the old sinful nature. "Therefore if any man be in Christ, he is a new creature: old things are passed away; behold, all things are become new" (II Corinthians 5:17). The new nature that counteracts the old is the Holy Spirit indwelling. This does not mean we are infallible or incapable of sinning. It does mean we have overcoming power dwelling within; the Spirit imparts to us the desire and power to live a holy life both inwardly and outwardly.

The process by which the Spirit separates us from sin and develops holiness in us is called sanctification. It consists of three parts: initial sanctification, continual sanctification, and final sanctification.

Initial Sanctification

The initial act of sanctification happens when we first receive the Holy Spirit baptism. Holiness is an attribute of God; no one can be holy apart from the Holy Spirit. Paul expressed, "And such were some of you: but ye are washed, but ye are sanctified, but ye are justified in the name of the Lord Jesus, and by the Spirit of our God" (I Corinthians 6:11). Sanctification is a supernatural act of God. Some never progress beyond this experience. Many eventually return to their old lifestyle. The apostle expressed, "But it is happened unto them according to the true proverb, The dog is turned to his own vomit again; and the sow that was washed to her wallowing in the mire" (II Peter 2:22).

Continued Sanctification

Those who remain in Christ experience a lifestyle of continued sanctification. The process of sanctification continues as the believer yields to the will of the Holy Spirit. The first church "...continued stedfastly in the apostles' doctrine" (Acts 2:42). The Holy Spirit continues the process of sanctification as we incorporate godly disciplines in our lives, practices that facilitate the work of the Holy Spirit.

1. Prayer. "And when they had prayed, the place was shaken where they were assembled together; and they were all filled with the Holy Ghost, and they spake the word of God with boldness" (Acts 4:31).

2. Obedience to the Word of God. "Sanctify them through thy truth: thy word is truth" John 17:17). That he might sanctify and cleanse it with the washing of water by the word" (Ephesians 5:26).

3. Obedience to spiritual leadership. "Obey them that have the rule over you, and submit yourselves: for they watch for your souls, as they that must give account, that they may do it with joy, and not with grief: for that is unprofitable for you" (Hebrews 1:17). "That ye submit yourselves unto such, and to every one that helpeth with us, and laboureth" (I Corinthians 16:16).

4. Christian fellowship. "And they continued stedfastly in the apostles' doctrine and fellowship, and in breaking of bread, and in prayers" (Acts 2:42). "But if we walk in the light, as he is in the light, we have fellowship one with another, and the blood of Jesus Christ his Son cleanseth us from all sin" (I John 1:7).

5. A repented lifestyle. "If we confess our sins, he is faithful and just to forgive us our sins, and to cleanse us from all unrighteousness" (I John 1:9). "If a man therefore purge himself from these, he shall be a vessel unto honour, sanctified, and meet for the masters use, and prepared unto every good work" (II Timothy 2:21).

6. Continual thanksgiving. "Rejoice evermore. Pray without ceasing. In every thing give thanks: for this is the will of God in Christ Jesus concerning you" (I Thessalonians 5:16-18). Lest we forget, the grateful heart keeps us toeing the mark. It may be tempting to have a drink while hanging out at the neighborhood bar, but it is difficult to pursue sin while praising the Savior.

Jesus explained we would be in the world but not of the world (John 17:11-16). Because we are in the world, we are exposed to many unclean things from which we must separate ourselves. Paul expressed, "Wherefore come out from among them, and be ye separate, saith the Lord, and touch not the unclean thing; and I will receive you" (II Corinthians 6:17). As Christians, since some habits are certainly detrimental to our health, we sense the need to refrain from such vices: smoking, drinking, and illicit drugs. Further, Paul warned against defiling God's dwelling place when he wrote, "If any man defile the temple of God, him shall God destroy; for the temple of God is holy, which temple ye are" (I Corinthians 3:17). To defile the physical body brings displeasure to the indwelling Holy Spirit. Still, even though we choose not to smoke, we inhale smoke-tainted air in restaurants and various places of business. While we separate ourselves as much as possible from worldly vices, we still encounter evil through the senses. The indwelling Holy Spirit sanctifies us in situations where contact with the world is unavoidable.

The Scripture proclaims, "But if we walk in the light, as he is in the light, we have fellowship one with another, and the blood of Jesus Christ his Son cleanseth us from all sin" (I John 1:7). This passage certainly refers to sinful acts we commit, but it specifically emphasizes the cleansing influence of the Holy Spirit in our lives. We are continually cleansed by Christ's atoning blood, even when we are not aware of the worldly influences that invade our lives through the senses.

Final Sanctification

The final stage of sanctification will take place at the catching away of the church into God's eternal presence. We will attain sinless perfection like Christ. Our physical bodies will be changed to be like Christ's glorified body. This work is permanent; it is for eternity. The child of God is prepared for this catching away without feeling absolutely perfect. Why? We have not yet experienced the final sanctification: the ultimate of sanctification, where the old nature is completely eradicated. Only the new nature will resurrect. This final sanctification is irreversible.

Though we may experience times of extreme displeasure with our spiritual walk, let us take courage. We must not despair because of weakness or because the old nature tries to regain authority in our lives. God's process for perfection is a three-stage process, and we are still in the second stage. God has not finished with us yet. We can and must press on to perfection.

Points of Discussion

Discuss the various stages of the three roads that are the options for a Christian who has sinned.

Why do we some choose the roads of the backslider and the hypocrite? What are the consequences?

Define and discuss the stages of sanctification. What are our responsibilities regarding sanctification?

CHAPTER 11

The Unpardonable Sin

Jesus said only one sin was unforgivable—blasphemy against the Holy Ghost (Matthew 12:31). Some worry they have committed this "unpardonable" sin. The devil certainly wants us to believe we have committed such evil, since it would leave us without hope. This is but another of his many tools to destroy our faith. Although we must not speak of this subject lightly, it is highly unlikely that the reader has committed this sin. Let's survey the reasons.

First, what is blasphemy against the Holy Ghost? This question brings a variety of responses. Three scriptural passages discuss this sin (Matthew 12:31; Mark 3:29; Luke 12:10). The Bible does not clarify exactly what this sin is, nor does it give a clear example of someone who has committed the sin, so it does not seem to be a commonly committed sin. Jesus did not accuse anyone of committing this sin but simply warned against blaspheming the Holy Ghost.

Webster's Dictionary defines blasphemy as "the act of insulting or showing contempt or lack of reverence for God." Blaspheming the Holy Ghost must he more than insulting God, however, for Jesus said blasphemy against the Son of man (God manifest in flesh—

Jesus Himself) could be forgiven. "And whosoever speaketh a word against the Son of man, it shall be forgiven him: but whosoever speaketh against the Holy Ghost, it shall not be forgiven him, neither in this world, neither in the world to come" (Matthew 12:32). Why this distinction? The answer must lie in the context that prompted these words of the Lord. Let's consider such.

The Pharisees accused Jesus of casting out demons by the power of the prince of demons (Mark 3:22). That is when Jesus warned them against blaspheming the Holy Ghost: "...because they said, He hath an unclean spirit" (Mark 3:30). They had associated the Spirit of Jesus (the Spirit of God) with the devil. Blasphemy against the Holy Ghost, then, must be more than backsliding. It is not only rejection of the Holy Spirit; it is accusing the Holy Spirit of being satanic. A person who does not understand the Bible should certainly speak circumspectly of the working of the Holy Spirit, but apparently someone would have to be very knowledgeable of the Holy Spirit before God holds them accountable for blasphemy against the Holy Spirit.

It is difficult to understand how someone who has experienced Christ's wonderful Spirit can speak against the Holy Spirit so forcefully as to blaspheme. Perhaps they have fallen into the previously mentioned state of apostasy where God has sent them strong delusion, and they have believed a lie (II Thessalonians 2:11). If so, no one can convince them otherwise. They can no longer believe the truth. Since they cannot see their own error, they feel no need for repentance. Because they feel no need for repentance, they do not seek forgiveness of God. This leaves them without hope of salvation. The impossibility of forgiveness comes, not because God refuses to forgive, but because of their lack of repentance for sin. Their disdain for God and the Bible places them in a position where they cannot recognize God's Spirit, and so God cannot deal with their heart regarding sin, and it is, therefore, impossible for them to be forgiven. They have cut God off and have not the conscience to allow Him back into their lives. Such an attitude as the religious leaders of Jesus' day had is quite different from those who get discouraged, question God, or backslide into sin.

The above explanation helps us to better understand some statements in the Book of Hebrews:

For it is impossible for those who were once enlightened, and have tasted of the heavenly gift, and were made partakers of the Holy Ghost, and have tasted the good word of God, and the powers of the world to come, if they shall fall away, to renew them again unto repentance; seeing they crucify to themselves the Son of God afresh, and put him to an open shame.

Hebrews 6:4-6

For if we sin willfully after that we have received the knowledge of the truth, there remaineth no more sacrifice for sins, but a certain fearful looking for of judgment and fiery indignation, which shall devour the adversaries. He that despised Moses' law died without mercy under two or three witnesses: Of how much sorer punishment, suppose ye, shall he be thought worthy, who hath trodden under foot the Son of God, and hath counted the blood of the covenant, wherewith he was sanctified, an unholy thing, and hath done despite unto the Spirit of grace.

Hebrews 10:26-29

Do these Scriptures mean the backslider has no hope for spiritual renewal? The answer is an emphatic "no." Still, to isolate these statements from the rest of Scripture would seemingly destroy any hope of forgiveness for the backslider or for the believer who has sinned. We must, therefore, interpret them in the light of other scriptural passages. The Bible teaches the availability of forgiveness to the believer who sins. "Brethren, if a man be overtaken in a fault, ye which are spiritual restore such an one" (Galatians 6:1). "If we confess our sins, he is faithful and just to forgive us our sins, and to cleanse us from all unrighteousness" (I John I:9). "My little children, these things write I unto you, that ye sin not. And if any man sin, we have an advocate with the Father, Jesus Christ the righteous" (I John 2:1).

These verses are in letters written to churches—to groups of believers who were already saved. John identified two reasons for writing his first epistle. First, he sought to instruct them in living an overcoming life: "...that ye sin not." Second, he wanted to assure those who had failed in their walk with Christ that there was still hope: "...if any man sin, we have an advocate." When Christ's disciples asked Him to teach them to pray, He included a request for forgiveness: "And forgive us our sins" (Luke 11:4). Since the Bible is the infallible Word of God, we cannot interpret the preceding passages as contradictory, with some teaching no hope of forgiveness and others teaching hope for forgiveness. Since the Bible as a whole definitely teaches that there is forgiveness, there must be a clearer understanding regarding those verses in the Book of Hebrews that speak of no hope. Again, we must look at the context.

The New Testament Book of Hebrews was written to Hebrew Christians. These Jewish converts to Christianity were in danger of relapsing into Judaism or "falling away" from the Christian faith. The writer pointed out that Christianity fulfills, surpasses, and replaces the ceremonial observances of the law, for the law was merely a "shadow of good things to come" (Hebrews 10:1; also see Colossians 2:17). Paul's letter to the Galatians further states, "The law was our schoolmaster to bring us unto Christ" (Galatians 3:24). The Thompson Chain-Reference Bible, in its analysis of Hebrews, states, "The chief doctrinal purpose of the writer was to show the transcendent glory of the Christian dispensation, as compared with that of the Old Testament." As we analyze Hebrews 6:4-6 and 10:26-30, we should note the phrases "fall away, crucify the Son of God afresh, no more sacrifice, trodden under foot the Son of God, counted the blood an unholy thing." Such phrases describe more than backsliding; they speak of renouncing Christ's atoning sacrifice at Calvary as sufficient for salvation. These Hebrew Christians were in danger of reaching backward to the Jewish law in order to obtain salvation. If they were to turn away from Calvary, their only source of salvation, and remain in that condition, forgiveness would be impossible. These passages in Hebrews were not written to pronounce judgment upon a Christian who had sinned, but they were written to warn against rejecting the plan and power of the cross for salvation.

There is no biblical example of God denying someone forgiveness for a repented sin. To the contrary, there are many admonitions to repent. It is true that Esau sought a place of repentance with tears but was rejected (Hebrews 12:17). This Scripture is insufficient proof of a repentant prayer being denied. Rather, Esau asked his father, Isaac, to repent—to change his mind—regarding the previously administered blessing of the family inheritance. Esau wanted his father to redo the ceremony and give him the blessing of the firstborn that Isaac had unknowingly given to Jacob, but it was too late (Genesis 27:34-38). The deed was done, and Isaac could not take it back (repent of it).

Moreover, a close examination of Esau's life reveals that God rejected his prayer because he came to the Lord on the wrong basis. He was like a sinner who is sorry he got caught but not sorry for his sin. Esau was sorry he had lost the blessing of the birthright, but there is no indication of an attempt to change his lifestyle. He had already sold his birthright to Jacob for a bowl of soup because he despised his birthright. Even when Esau pleaded for the blessing, he was not willing to pay the price of a life submitted to God. He was a fornicator and a profane person (Hebrews 12:16). He did not repent of his sin nor attempt to stop sinning; he only sought the blessing that Isaac bestowed upon Jacob.

If Esau had come to the Lord with the proper motive—as a sinner needing forgiveness—God would have forgiven him. Regrettably, Esau did not. He apparently died an unrepentant, unhappy rebel.

In short, the Bible proclaims that we can receive forgiveness of sins. We do not have to bear the burden of guilt for the rest of our lives because of sins committed in the past. The Lord has already carried the weight of our sin and guilt on Calvary.

Not only can we have forgiveness for our sins, we can have peace. That was the message surrounding Christ's birth. The angels sang unto the shepherds, proclaiming peace on earth (Luke 2:14). Jesus promised His disciples, "Peace I leave with you, my peace I give unto you" (John 14:27). Paul wrote, "Be careful (anxious) for nothing; but in every thing by prayer and supplication with thanksgiving let your requests be made known unto God. And the peace of God, which passeth all understanding, shall keep your hearts and minds through Christ Jesus" (Philippians 4:6-7). Christ offers us peace, including freedom from the guilt of past sin. Repentance and acceptance of forgiveness through faith bring this peace.

How can this be when God's justice demands that the guilty pay? True, God's judgment for sin is death, but I John 2:2 explains that Christ is the propitiation for our sins. To propitiate means: "to atone for, reduce the anger of, to win the favor of, to appease the one offended." In other words, Christ died in our place and paid the penalty for our sins. This satisfies the just requirements of God's law and allows Him to pardon our sin without violating His law. The eternal God viewed Christ's death as sufficient enough to turn away His judicial wrath against our sins.

When we believe on Christ and obey His gospel regarding the means of acquiring salvation, Christ's death applies to our debt of sin. At baptism in the name of Christ, it is as if we had died for our debt of sin. "Buried with him in baptism, wherein also ye are risen with him through the faith of the operation of God, who hath raised him from the dead" (Colossians 2:12). Contrariwise, we do not literally die, for Christ already died on Calvary for our sins. It's akin to the law of double jeopardy—you can't be tried for the same crime once acquitted. At Calvary, Christ paid our debt of sin by His death; He refuses to allow us to pay for the same crime the second time. We identify with Christ's death by the new birth experience of water baptism and Holy Spirit infilling. If a Christian sins, he must repent of that sin. In so doing, he obtains God's forgiveness. Then he must accept this forgiveness by faith and thank Christ for suffering in his stead. Since Christ has forgiven him, he must forgive himself. Then he can continue to grow in Christ. Not only has God provided for forgiveness of sin, He has also provided for us to be overcomers.

The Book of I John presents three progressive steps of spiritual growth for the Christian. First, it encourages the one who has fallen prey to sin to repent, for Christ will forgive (I John 1:9). Next, it encourages the Christian to overcome sin (I John 2:1). Finally, it describes potential of the Christian to conquer sin in his life. When a Christian completely follows the born-again nature, he can live a life free from habitual sinful habits. "Whosoever abideth in him sinneth not: whosoever sinneth hath not seen him, neither known him. Whosoever is born of God doth not commit sin; for his seed remaineth in him: and he cannot sin, because he is born of God" (I John 3:6, 9).

Does this Scripture mean that if one sins he has never been born again? Alternatively, does it mean that Christ will totally ignore sin committed by the born-again believer—as if no sin he commits after conversion is considered sin? In light of the rest of the Bible, the answer to both of these questions is negative. Rather, John taught that if someone professes salvation but continues to live in sin, he has not truly received a full realization of God's will for the believer; he lacked something in his spiritual understanding. If someone is saved, as long as he follows the new nature of the Spirit rather than the old nature of the flesh, he will not commit sin. In short, the Christian who is walking after the Spirit will not habitually sin.

These passages from I John have reference to the maturation process of a Christian in which the Christian progressively overcomes sin. We begin as babes in Christ. There is a correlation to the natural growth of an individual and the spiritual growth. The spiritual infant must grow into spiritual maturity. The progress begins with the original blessing of salvation. When the Christian sins, he can repent and receive forgiveness from God. Eventually he can achieve complete victory over that area of sin. Interestingly, John did not command complete victory over sin until he first assured us of forgiveness for failure. Still, he did not leave us satisfied with failure, but he points us in the direction of victory. Not only is forgiveness for sin available, but victory over sin is also possible.

Points of Discussion

Discuss the unpardonable sin. Why is it highly unlikely you have committed this sin?

Why did Jesus warn the Pharisees regarding the unpardonable sin?

Discuss what the Bible meant regarding Esau not finding repentance.

When is our prayer similar to that of Esau's?

CHAPTER 12

The Temptation of Christ

W hat would have happened to the human race if Christ could and would have yielded to Satan's temptations? On this question we can speculate; however, we do not have to do so. Christ was victorious! Both Matthew 4 and Luke 4 record Christ's victory over Satan's attempt to get Him to succumb to temptation. This confrontation was an epochal battle in history. It was not the first, nor will it be the last, assault of the wicked upon the just. That struggle symbolized all the temptations of the devil, both past and future. The outcome gives the believer assurance of victory over sin. The temptation of Christ is prophetic of Satan's final defeat. Jesus proclaimed, "Be of good cheer; I have overcome the world" (John 16:33).

It is instructive to analyze both the timing and the method of Satan's temptation of Christ. This gives insight in handling the temptations Satan brings to us.

First, the timing of Christ's temptations is important. "Then was Jesus led up of the Spirit into the wilderness to be tempted of the devil" (Matthew 4:1). "Then" refers to the time immediately after His baptism and the public inauguration of His ministry. Someone once said, "The seasons of highest spiritual exaltation are often followed by those of greatest moral peril..."[17] A spiritual walk with God does not eliminate temptation; it simply assures victory. This is what Paul meant when he wrote, "Walk in the Spirit, and ye shall not fulfil the lust of the flesh" (Galatians 5:l6). Walking after the Spirit does not eliminate temptation; instead, it makes us more conscious of imperfections that need correction. Neither is Satan intimidated by an inspirational church service; he may view it as an opportunity to tempt when we least expect it.

The story of a newly converted young couple will illustrate this point. Their enthusiasm and testimony for Christ was thrilling. God had delivered them from the clutches of deepest sin, and the future seemed so bright. Each week they met in their home with their pastor for a private Bible study. They were so eager to learn and grow in Christ.

Suddenly it happened. Without any warning or even a hint of brewing adversity, the man lost his job. Due to problems from the past, his wife left him. If the man had been still living in sin, he could have accepted such setbacks somewhat easier, but he had just allowed Christ into his life. He thought things should get better, but they got worse, or at least they seemed worse.

It did not take much spiritual perception to realize what was happening. The battle to reclaim his soul had started. Satan wasted no time in opening fire against these new converts, and he used some heavy artillery.

The pastor assured the husband his experience with Christ was genuine and this was why Satan attacked. By faith the husband accepted this counsel and determined to maintain his newfound faith. The battle didn't turn around overnight, but the end result was victory. Over a year's time, his marriage solidified. He worked odd jobs until, miraculously, he received a job he had previously tried to obtain numerous times. He had wanted a particular job driving a truck, but in order to get the job he was required to take an expensive training course that would keep him out of church for ten consecutive Sundays. He did not have the money for the training, and he certainly needed to be in church. God intervened, and the man was hired as a dockhand. A few weeks later he was backing trucks up to the dock. Eventually, without having to take the extensive training course away from home, he acquired the hands-on training necessary for the job.

It's significant for the new convert to understand there's no exemption from temptation. The enemy doesn't offer immunity to the inexperienced; he views this as opportunity to attack. The tempter is emotionally hardened, with an abortionist's mentality.

Still, there is no set pattern for the attack of Satan. He attacks both the immature and the seasoned. Since his attacks often come without warning, the Scripture shows examples of a spiritual warning system preceding Satan's appearance. The prophets often warned of impending danger. The Lord warned Cain, "Sin lieth at the door..." (Genesis 4:7). Jesus told Simon Peter, "Satan hath desired to have you" (Luke 22:31). Peter remembered the warning after he had denied Christ. Many believers can recall a time when, through a sermon, a verse of Scripture, or an impression from the indwelling Spirit, God forewarned them of a situation that could have been very detrimental to their Christian walk.

As a pastor, I have experienced the urging of the Spirit to warn individuals of impending danger. Some heeded the warning and escaped Satan's snare, but unfortunately some did not. One case is particularly tragic. I was suddenly impressed in an unusual manner that a young man I pastored planned to move to a distant city but that he should be discouraged from doing so. A few minutes later, the young man arrived at my office to announce his plans. Hoping to not sound selfish by encouraging him to remain in the local church, I expressed what I felt in the Spirit. The young man did not heed what proved to be a warning from the Lord. He proceeded headstrong with his plan. Not long after that, he stopped attending church and eventually denied the faith.

Satan is very unpredictable. The Bible describes him as a serpent. A snake usually is not the aggressor but protects itself when endangered. As Christians, we can certainly put Satan on the defensive (James 4:7). Still, the Bible also describes Satan as an aggressor. "Be sober, be vigilant; because your adversary the devil, as a roaring lion, walketh about, seeking whom he may devour" (I Peter 5:8). A lion does not generally fight to defend; he attacks to destroy.

The most likely time for Satan to tempt us is at a spiritually low point in our lives. In particular, a lack of consistent prayer, personal

Bible reading, and cooperate worship make us more susceptible to temptation. We discussed these in chapter six of this book.

Seniority in living for God does not protect someone against temptation. King David was probably seventy years old when "Satan stood up against Israel, and provoked David to number Israel" (I Chronicles 21:1). In short, if we ask when temptation is likely to come, the answer is any time. Paul's instruction to the church may well have had this in mind.

> Pray without ceasing. In every thing give thanks: for this is the will of God in Christ Jesus concerning you. Quench not the Spirit. Despise not prophesyings. Prove all things; hold fast that which is good. Abstain from all appearance of evil. And the very God of peace sanctify you wholly; and I pray God your whole spirit and soul and body be preserved blameless unto the coming of our Lord Jesus Christ.
>
> I Thessalonians 5:17-23

The second question to investigate regarding the temptation of Christ is how does Satan tempt us? At the outset, we must realize that Satan is not always personally present at each temptation. Remember, he is not omnipresent. Moreover, we cannot truthfully say, "The devil made me do it." He is definitely our tempter, but we associate all temptations with him only because he was the original tempter of the human race. We should note that Satan directly tempted Eve, not Adam; Adam's temptation came from his wife. Further, after the Fall, our nature took on selfish desires of the flesh.

Prior to the Fall, man was not plagued by the many temptations of the world today. Man was responsible to keep but one commandment: "Of the tree of the knowledge of good and evil, thou shalt not eat of it" (Genesis 2:17). Satan could not entice Adam and Eve to curse, lie, steal, or lust; their innocence sheltered them from these sins. They did not have to fight the sinful nature with its innate desire and compulsion to sin; they only faced an external attack from Satan in the form of a suggestion to eat the forbidden fruit. Satan attacked them in the only area in which they were accountable. They yielded, breaking the command of God and polluting their innocent nature with sin.

After the Fall, man became vulnerable to other areas of temptation. John described the temptations of the world today as "…the lust of the flesh, and the lust of the eye, and the pride of life" (I John 2:16). Before the Fall, his innocence sheltered him from these areas of accountability and vulnerability. After his disobedience, these became part of man's sinful nature. Now, not only can Satan tempt us by external means, but also our senses have become accountable, and we must now combat internal fleshly desires. This is the "Adamic nature" which all receive at birth. We do not have to learn about sin; the desire for sinfulness is alive within us at birth. At some point as a child, we shed innocence and take on accountability for our decisions and actions.

Becoming a Christian doesn't remove the Adamic nature; rather, the old nature's influence is diluted and becomes manageable. A greater nature becomes resident within us when we become a born again believer. God doesn't consider us sinful because inward desires of the old nature remain. He views us as holy, controlling the natural desires through the Holy Spirit and refusing to mentally entertain or indulge them in our actions. However, if we don't control these desires, they will result in sin.

In studying the temptation of Christ, we discover three ways in which Satan tempted Him: with physical desires, presumptuous trust, and personal ambition.

Physical Desires

The first temptation of the Lord was in the realm of physical desires. A common trick of Satan is to entice men to satisfy innocent desires in wrong ways. Natural desires are not sinful in themselves but can become traps of the devil. Satan uses natural desires to tempt man. The Greek word translated as "lust" does not necessarily refer to sinful desires only. It involves any excessiveness in gratifying natural physical desires. It is not wrong to eat food to satisfy hunger, nor even to enjoy the taste of food. After all, God created us with taste buds, and He created food with different flavors. The desire to eat and enjoy food is natural. Excessive eating, however, is gluttony (Numbers 11:32-34; Deuteronomy 21:20; Proverbs 23:I-3, 21). Eating is a natural desire, but overeating can lead to sin. Satan always pushes us beyond the natural and permissive mark. It is for us to recognize the difference and to live on the side of moderation instead of overindulgence regarding a natural and life-preserving appetite.

Satan first tempted Christ by challenging Him to turn stones into bread. After forty days without food, Jesus' natural reaction was ravenous hunger. His desire for food was innocent; in fact, He needed food to sustain His life. Moreover, the act of turning stone into bread in itself was not sinful. Why then did Jesus refuse to resort to the miraculous? If He had complied with the suggestion of the devil, He would have aligned His will with Satan's plan. He would have lost touch with the day-to-day struggle of humanity. If He could not withstand the natural pains of hunger, He certainly would not withstand the inflicted pains of Calvary. Somewhere during the long and torturous ordeal of Calvary, He would have capitulated to His will, and He would have abandoned the will of the Father. It would have defeated the purpose of Incarnation to use the power of God to satisfy physical desires and to escape the feeling of humanities' infirmities.

Christians must be careful to control the desires of the flesh. Self-indulgence in one area can lead to greater self-indulgence in another area until finally the person loses control—not only over natural desires, but over sinful desires as well. A person generally does not fall into sin suddenly; it is a gradual process. He gives in to fleshly desires by spending more time in seeking pleasure than in seeking God through prayer and Bible reading. As a result, he gradually loses control of the flesh. Eventually the desires of the flesh become uncontrollable. Unless he realizes his condition, repents, and renews his Christian commitment, he will surely fail God.

It is important to note that Jesus had just spent forty days in prayer and fasting. The end result, He was weak physically but strong spiritually. With each temptation, He combatted Satan with the Christian's greatest defense—"It is written." It is imperative that we, too, pray continually and know what the Word of God says.

In Christ's temptation we recognize the significance of prayer. Jesus was our ultimate example of victorious living. Still, some we look up to as our example fail. It is certainly discouraging to the laity when a minister of the gospel falls prey to temptation. The son of a preacher who fell into sin once remarked, "Dad never did have much of a prayer life." Paul admonished us to "pray without ceasing" (I Thessalonians 5:17). Jesus is our ultimate example of the significance of prayer in order to overcome our fleshly desires.

Christ offered instruction in overcoming: "Watch and pray, that ye enter not into temptation: the spirit indeed is willing, but the flesh is weak" (Matthew 26:41). Watching includes knowing God's will and being able to recognize Satan's traps. What better method of watching is there than to have a genuine knowledge of the Bible? Christ used His knowledge of Scripture to combat Satan's distortion of Scripture. Satan made reference to Old Testament Scripture when he tempted Christ to turn stone into bread, but Christ interpreted Scripture when he proclaimed, "It is written, Man shall not live by bread alone, but by every word that proceedeth out of the mouth of God" (Matthew 4:4). The psalmist declared, "Thy word have I hid in mine heart, that I might not sin against thee" (Psalm 119:11). It is foolish of any Christian to think he can overcome temptation without much prayer and Bible reading.

We should also note the importance of fasting, for Jesus fasted forty days before His temptation. The natural inclination is to think ourselves stronger when we eat, but food only creates physical strength, not spiritual strength. Ironically, we are stronger spiritually when we fast. God does not need to see us go hungry. He receives no personal gratification from our pain, nor can our sacrifice earn anything from God. What, then, is the purpose of fasting? It is a way of disciplining the mind to say "no" to the desires of the flesh. We must condition ourselves to control the flesh and its desires. All three disciplines—prayer, Bible reading, and fasting—need to be a consistent part of our Christian walk.

Presumptuous Trust

The second area of the temptation of Christ concerned the intellect. Satan tested Christ's knowledge of the Scriptures. He tempted Christ with presumptuous trust based on a distortion of Scripture, suggesting it doesn't matter how dangerously close to the world you live because God has promised to rescue you. Satan challenged Jesus to throw Himself off the pinnacle of the temple since the Old Testament promised angelic protection for God's people.

Satan often resorts to Scriptural quotations. It is easy for a Bible-quoting minister of the devil to mislead the biblically unlearned. Many false religions use Scripture to substantiate their beliefs. To avoid such deception, we must become students of the entire Bible. We dare not allow the adversary to use an isolated verse of Scripture to bring confusion into our lives. As a pastor, one of the saddest encounters I have is with parishioners who hang their hats on an isolated Scripture and abandon the general truth of Scripture. Jesus was able to resist this temptation of Satan because He knew the Word in its entirety. He was able to explain the passage Satan misused by quoting another passage: "Thou shalt not tempt the Lord thy God" (Matthew 4:7).

Satan tempts men to increase their knowledge by experiences that needlessly endanger their physical and spiritual lives. He tempts teenagers to experiment with sex, drugs, and reckless driving. He tempts adults to misuse credit, to live beyond their means, and to acquire habits that endanger their health. Often he tempts people to undertake tasks beyond their ability to perform. The list seems endless.

Of course, to please God we must live by faith. The adversary uses this principle to tempt us into areas of vulnerability. An extreme example is using the Scripture to promote the practice of snake handling: "They shall take up serpents; and if they drink any deadly thing, it shall not hurt them; they shall lay hands on the sick, and they shall recover" (Mark 16:18). A more pertinent example of compromising Scripture is to use isolated Scriptures to justify social drinking: "Drink no longer water, but use a little wine for thy stomach's sake and thine often infirmities. (I Timothy 5:3). And of course the adherents throw in Christ's miracle of water into wine. These Scriptures are flagrantly misused, overlooking the numerous Scriptures that warn of alcohol's devastation to individuals, not to mention the current statistics and tragic examples of alcohol's societal wreckage. We avoid a host of Scriptures promoting responsibility and moderation, and we plunge head first into the storm clouds of stupidity, assuming we are walking by faith. "Cast yourself down," Satan cajoled Christ, "for the Scripture promises God will rescue you. Take the leap of faith and oblige God of His promises." Using Scripture in an attempt to obligate God to rescue us from overindulgences—alcoholism, bankruptcy, wrecks—is not faith. It is the sin of presumption. Samson fell into this trap. Because God had delivered him before, Samson assumed God would always be there. He treated the Spirit of God like a switch for a light bulb—something to turn on and off at will. Samson disobeyed his parents, his conscience, and his God, yet he awoke from a nap on Delilah's knees expecting God to be standing at attention in the corner. He was unaware God's Spirit had grievously left the scene, leaving him to his own capability.

We need not fear that God will forsake us while we are living for Him and doing our best to follow His Word. If we purposefully put ourselves in unnecessary danger, however, we have no guarantee of divine deliverance. "The Lord is merciful and gracious, slow to anger, and plenteous in mercy" (Psalms 103:8), but He is not a puppet on a string.

Too often we learn this lesson by experience. A number of years ago, I attended a rally designed to raise money for a New York City crusade. The service, particularly the sermon, was very stirring. As a plea went forth for a sacrificial offering, I willingly gave my entire savings, confident that God would replenish it. There was one small hitch: the money in the savings was money I owed the government for tax. In retrospect, it was not my money. It was "Caesar's money," and I should render it to him. It was the miracle coin found in the fish's mouth (Matthew 17:27), but I spent it on a meal on my way to the tax collector. After all, if God did it once, He could do it again. Over the years, God has certainly blessed me abundantly, but this one particular time I had to learn an important lesson. The savings was not really mine, but money designated for taxes. I thought that giving the money would bring a financial blessing and somehow obligate God to give back the money before the due date. God did not. I suffered the embarrassment of sending in a tax return with money owed that I could not pay until later.

Why did not God supply the money? First of all, God did not want Caesar's money; He wanted my money. So I should have given a smaller amount of money that belonged to me. Second, any blessing should have gone to the government, for it was the government's money. Third, what were the true motives for giving? Did I give because I wanted to see the Kingdom of God prosper, or did I give because of peer pressure? Fourth, if God had blessed the gift, He would have sanctioned giving away something that did not truly belong to the donor.

There's a danger in isolating Scriptures—picking and choosing at one's fancy. It was during my teen years, and I'd only been saved a short time, when I first read the Scripture, "If ye shall ask any thing in my name, I will do it" (John 14:14). This sounded to me like the good life. My first opportunity to use this miracle verse came during a Latin class. The teacher announced a test for the next day. Seizing upon this opportunity, I breathed a prayer of promise: "Lord, don't let me fail the test." I left my Latin textbook in my locker and spent the evening doing what I wanted, certainly not studying for the next day's test. During Latin class the next day, the teacher announced the test was postponed until the next day. I smiled to myself and repeated my previous prayer. The next day the teacher announced she wasn't giving the test as usual. Instead, she had the class stand, and she began asking a series of questions—obviously the ones on the test. When a student gave the correct answer, he was permitted to sit. I went through the entire series of questions without one correct answer. How humiliating! Though, per my prayer, I never failed the test, for we were not given a grade for the unusual experiment, but neither did I pass. I learned the lesson the hard way. Prayer isn't a crutch for slothfulness, and the Bible has a bunch of Scriptures regarding slothfulness. Too bad I hadn't read those along with the Scriptures regarding faith.

Small infractions lead to greater ones. The types of actions described above can lead to more serious actions. They can lead to someone taking money from a business petty cash fund for personal use with the intention of replacing the borrowed money, or filling out a tax form without substantiating deductions. Many have committed such sins. They usually started, however, with something smaller.

As another example, let us suppose someone has a monthly income of two thousand dollars and monthly expenses of two thousand dollars. He should not, by faith, buy a new car requiring monthly payments of an additional three hundred dollars, for he has no right to expect God to supply the additional money needed. God is not obligated to bless our overspending. To the contrary, this could well fall into the category of tempting God through presumptuous trust.

Operating out of presumptuous trust—immature faith—may lead to far greater problems. The additional expense for the car would probably end in repossession or may require the person to work overtime or a second job. This, in turn, could take him away from family activities, prayer, and church attendance. With the physical exhaustion that comes with extra work, misunderstandings could easily develop in the home. All of these could have been prevented if he had lived within his means—he couldn't afford the new car—instead of tempting God through presumptuous trust.

Personal Ambition

The third area of the temptation Christ faced was personal ambition. We all must contend with the challenge to define between God's will and our personal ambitions, which may fall outside God's will for us or are premature in God's timing. Satan offered Christ the kingdoms of the world if Christ would worship him. He was actually offering Christ that which already belonged to Him. Christ would receive complete dominion in God's timing, but Satan offered it to Him prematurely and with a condition—fall down and worship me. Not only did Christ refuse the condition of giving allegiance to Satan, but also He was willing to wait upon the kingdom that would someday be His. The Apostle Paul encouraged us to think as Jesus thought in this area: "Let this mind be in you, which was also in Christ Jesus" (Philippians 2:5). How did Jesus think? "Who, being in the form of God, thought it not robbery to be equal with God: but made himself of no reputation, and took upon Him the form of a servant" (Philippians 2:6-7). Christ thought as a servant—not a servant by birth or misfortune, but a servant by choice.

The Old Testament gave instructions for the treatment of a Hebrew slave. After six years the slave could go free. If for some reason he did not want to depart from his master, he could remain a servant. As a sign that he chose to serve his master for life, he had his ear lobe bored through with an awl. He became a servant by choice. Such was the attitude of Christ. He could have called down angels to destroy the entire Roman army, acquiring the kingdom prematurely, but He did not. He remained on the cross by choice.

A servant's attitude is different from the free man's attitude. The servant does not expect too much. He does not argue about rights.

His giving precedes and exceeds his receiving. The servant works to please his master and not himself. He does not complain but gives thanks. Christ became a servant by choice, and He remained so until God's timing for elevation.

Too often we do not wait upon the blessings of God. We fail to "seek...first the kingdom of God" (Matthew 6:33). Because of this, many do not receive the intended blessings from the Lord, and some even miss heaven itself. We must remember that Satan is not beyond offering things he cannot deliver. He may even prematurely offer blessings that God intends to give at a later date. We must also remember that Satan gives nothing for free. The price he demands is that we "fall down and worship him" (Matthew 4:9).

Having ambition is not wrong in itself. We should always seek to do our best in whatever we do; however, we must not let personal ambition overshadow the will of God for our lives. God's blessings do not come too early, but they will always come on time, if we are willing to wait.

The Departure of Satan

This final point relative to Christ's temptation is of utmost importance. After the three tests, Matthew records, "Then the devil leaveth him" (Matthew 4:1 1). Some see this as permanent victory. At this point they are ready to celebrate or at least to relax their guard against Satan. The gospel writer Luke says, however, "The devil... departed from him for a season" (Luke 4:13). This Scripture shares additional information—Satan only abandoned "this" scheme. He would return with another approach. Momentary reprieve from Satan's attacks are just that—momentary. He will be back. For Christ, a battle had been won, but the war was not yet over. Kenneth Wuest explains that the Greek wording in the Gospel of Luke indicates "a standing off from."[18] In other words, Satan did not acknowledge defeat but withdrew a distance to reevaluate the situation and await another opportunity to attack.

For this reason we must never let down our guard against temptation. Satan and his temptations are always near, awaiting a chance to attack again. Paul wrote, "For we are not ignorant of his devices" (II Corinthians 2:11). Out of concern for the Corinthians, he again wrote, "But I fear, lest by any means, as the serpent beguiled Eve through his subtilty, so your minds should be corrupted from the simplicity that is in Christ" (II Corinthians 11:3). As the preacher of old expressed, "There is no new thing under the sun" (Ecclesiastes 1:9). The same devil that beguiled Eve, tested Job, stood up against David, and desired Simon Peter is still loose today. He is a continual adversary whom we cannot destroy; however, we certainly do not have to yield to him.

We must beware of the error of concentrating only on "big" temptations. The grand, personal attack from Satan himself may never happen to us, but our lives will always be susceptible to those "little foxes, that spoil the vines" (Song of Solomon 2:15). We may need to expend great effort to cope with mountainous problems that can destroy our lives overnight, but we must not neglect smaller issues such as bad feelings towards the boss or uncontrollable anger at the driver who honks his horn for no good reason. David conquered Goliath with one stone, but he started into the battle with five stones. He was ready in case he missed the first time; he was also ready for an attack by anyone else.

This book has given some instructions for defense against Satan's attacks. These instructions are certainly not exhaustive. It is my hope they will assist you in overcoming sin. You can be confident in your Christian walk, for God's Word promises victory over temptation for those who submit to God and resist the devil. You can be an overcomer!

Points of Discussion

Why did Christ submit to being tempted of Satan?

Discuss the defenses Christ used to combat Satan's temptation.

In comparison to the temptations of Christ, discuss the ways in which Satan tempts us in each of the categories: physical desires, presumptuous trust, and personal ambition.

What are some of the "little foxes" we must be on guard against?

How can we apply the defenses Christ used against Satan to combat our temptations?

Author Acknowledgments

With gratitude I acknowledge the wonderful people who made this book possible.

I am indebted to Tammy Fisher for her editing skills, Aaron Arrowood for his creative cover design, Michael Clark for website assistance, Kenny Noble who walks me through technical issues and gives pointers on writing, and a special friend who does the layout but refuses to allow his name in print.

I appreciate Mark Blackburn of PPH for releasing the copyright of the original *Overcoming Temptation* and allowing me reprint rights.

Also, I extend special thanks to the Woodsong Publishing team for putting my fifth title into print.

The team at Lightning Source is always so courteous and helpful.

Further, I appreciate the wonderful Tabernacle Church Family in Seymour, IN who allows me the freedom to write and cheers me on in the process.

Moreover, I recognize I need not write were it not for the gracious readers who purchase my books. Thank you!

Finally, I hope this book honors Christ and that it inspires someone to continue on the Christian journey.

(Endnotes)

Chapter 1

1   Eugene H. Peterson, Scripture taken from *The Message.* Copyright © 1993, 1994, 1995, 1996, 2000, 2001, 2002. Used by permission of NavPress Publishing Group.

2   Attributed to Abe Gubegna, Ethiopia, author and journalist, 1944 -1980. Quoted by Christopher McDougall, Born to Run: A Hidden Tribe, Superathletes, and the Greatest Race the World Has Never Seen, (Vintage Books, New York), 2011.

Chapter 2

3   James Strong, *Strong's Exhaustive Concordance of the Bible,* Hendrickson Publishers

4   Super Snakes, National Geographic for Kids, Issue 422, page 17.

Chapter 3

5   Kenneth Wuest, *Word Studies in the Greek, Volume III,* (Grand Rapids: Eerdmans, 1973), 15.

6   Ibid., 17.

7   Donna Snodgrass, "Stress," Indianapolis Star, October 14, 1979).

Chapter 5

8   Kenneth Wuest, *Word Studies in the Greek, Volume III,* (Grand Rapids: Eerdmans, 1973), 126.

9   Nathaniel Urshan, Pastor Calvary Tabernacle, Indianapolis, IN; General Superintendent, United Pentecostal Church International, 1920-2005.

10   Will Durant, *Caesar and Christ, A History of Roman Civilization & of Christianity from their Beginnings to A.D. 325,* (1944).

11   Article, *The Daily Walk,* (January 1980).

12   Article by Hans Selye, (Psychology Today, March, 1978).

Chapter 6

13   Elizabeth Kübler-Ross, Noted for her stages of death model, Switzerland, (1926-204).

14   Winston Churchill, British Prime Minister, (1874-1965).

Chapter 8

15   Charles Durham, Temptation, Help for Struggling Christians, (Intervarsity Press,1982), 37.

Chapter 9

16   Quoted by Edward Hindson, *Aids to Understanding the Holy Bible*, (1968), 3.

Chapter 11

17   Charles Rosenbury Erdman, *The Gospel of Matthew*, (The Westminster Press, Philadelphia, 1921), 38.

18   Kenneth Wuest, *Word Studies in the Greek, Volume III*, (Grand Rapids: Eerdmans, 1973).